CUTBANK
85

CutBank is published biannually at the University of Montana by graduate students in the Creative Writing Program. Publication is funded and supported by the Associated Students of Montana, the Pleiades Foundation, the Second Wind Reading Series, Humanities Montana, Tim O'Leary, Michelle Cardinal, William Kittredge, Annick Smith, Truman Capote Literary Trust, Sponsors of the Fall Writer's Opus, the Department of English, the Creative Writing Program, Kevin Canty, Judy Blunt, Karin Schalm, Michael Fitzgerald & Submittable, and our readers & donors.

Subscriptions are $15 per year + $3 for subscriptions outside of North America. Make checks payable to *CutBank* or shop online at www.cutbankonline.org/subscribe.

Our reading period is September 15 - February 1. Complete submission guidelines are available online.

All correspondence to:
CutBank
English Department, LA 133
University of Montana
Missoula, MT 59812

Printed by McNaughton & Gunn.

CUTBANK EIGHTY-FIVE

EDITOR-IN-CHIEF
Billy Wallace

ONLINE MANAGING EDITOR
Kate Barrett

SOCIAL MEDIA EDITOR
Nate Duke

FICTION EDITORS
Alicia Bones
Read Trammel

POETRY EDITORS
Jolene Brink
Charlie Decker
Sierra Jacobs
Eve Kenneally

NONFICTION EDITORS
Riley Gillan
Stefan Olson

EDITORIAL INTERN
Vanessa Mattfield

READERS
Grace Arenas, Sarah Aronson, Kate Barrett, Mack Basham,
Anna Blackburn, Linnea Blank, Max Boyd, Renee Bra-
num, Nate Duke, Rebecca Durham, Brian Groh, Kristina
Johnson, KJ Kern, Vanessa Mattfield, Zoe May, Lisbet
Portman, Stephanie Pushaw, Zac Raasch, Hamish Rickett,
Jeanie Riess, Nicole Roche, Claire Voris.

COVER
Illustration by Margaret Darling

CONTENTS

IN STILL

& in conjure we learn intimate
molecules heap in design to
this wide open, let's all
stammer as we say *everything*,
word of worlds; both wide &
otherwise; word in thalamus
caught in kingdoms of air,
thought, & ink requires all &
nothing of science

to build inside a body/outside
a body; we all in string to;

lamps of energy burning & in
burn.

To be peasant of language; to
draw breath & what exhales
paints us; a *new* new; say
swaddle; how the petal devotes
to flower as flower; how in
night, first, you hear the leaves
release from the aspen; how
the whisper devours you,
unable in sun's westerly crawl
to forgive the light, when you,
yes you, in still, in
still.

Body Language

When my father's right leg began to tremor
we couldn't pretend not to notice anymore.

> I found a tree with a knothole
> large enough to hold my whole body

then climbed inside.

> It isn't enough *to be there when it happens*
> *and write it down*

but first to cultivate
the right shade of blindness.

> I had to cross a little wooden bridge,

see the groundcovering
all wrecked with rain.

> I plunged my thumbs
> into the tree's soft interior

not for learning to love its marrow

> but to watch the bits of wood
> strip and heave like a downed deer.

THEORY OF EVERYTHING

Grandmother, croon your ruinous tenor
through the valley of the damned. Sow long furrows
for the Boot [*its laces so gruesomely*]
that broke your fishbowl, stomped your fish's
tiny lungs. On the train they're branded
chattels and given each
one greasy soap. This is television. The choir rises
to executive level and lawyers swap [*key party!*]
and bag Manhattan. This is *game show*, bang-bang, ask the dodo,
ask the noble ungulates and the large, free-roaming mammals
of North America. Ask the buffalo what they know
in their long, long bones. The slaughter
is just beginning. Draw near then, Family, behold
this prehistoric cup, its aura of beauty and devastating
wonder. Let it soothe you a Little Song of Nothing
about volcanic outgassing and accretion
from the solar nebula. We'll go to America,
where they practice chemical gelding of starlets
violated as children [*but the spirit forbears*]
and everything you believe has already been,
harvested from arcana and oracle and dream-catcher
and Tarot and corralled into blinding amphitheaters
and divined to be Not
Enough. And your fate is called.
And it is called: Rodeo.

COMPREHENSIBLE TERMS

After Mary Biddinger

I knew it was time to begin again. The stark
fissure between our bodies. Days spent trenching

through the muck. We shared the same
topography of heart and liver, but we called

it up in different words. Basic elements of
life became uncomfortable. Everywhere

I turned, you had irradiated a chair or footstool,
afraid I would stop there permanently. Even

the mattress was toxic. Friends who came
wanting to know what language you were

speaking went away disappointed. There was
no dictionary for this brand of evasion.

I hunted recipes that might convert your
speech, or mine. A different, rented syntax:

the smooth structures of someone else. Once,
you'd drink and the horizon would bow.

A coterie of planets behind you. With me you
were a sad tangle of syllables. We fabricated

the scene of your interpretation, each of us
alone, with descriptors we could understand.

AND YET, CONSIDER THE GLOAMING

which suggests we have on our hands
a poetic twilight.

You say *that beautiful, that cool,* and
I wonder if you mean the dusk or

me, somehow – I guess I know
how I fit along the hem of your memory.

This is how it feels when something
important doesn't happen –

darkness drops Octoberly, certainly
another word for it could be serenity.

I can see everything despite the dark
(except my rolling eyes).

You yoke for it, want a statement –
my windbent whisper: fuck you.

TWICE

once i am
beside my body
      twice like pines
      full of silence
once a song
twice a broken piano

How Medea Remembers Jason

Mornings, she prunes the herb garden, cuts leaves and stems
to wash by hand. Hasn't forged a curse in years, too late grown
mindful. But didn't they bend, yielding to one another
so they might burn the reeds around the house in shield circles,
the only crops that would flourish? What remains: his noise-lack
in the kitchen, early riser. Gathering the green in her shirtfront,
laying the color out, she moves alone among the rooms where he
does not reside. This house is a heartfloor, open wound.
See how she lifts the needle slow from the record, considers
replacing, drops it back. Do not think about the scorching
of his lover's limbs, her handiwork. See how she wakes at night,
steps outside to touch the bark of their tree. Everything
she was made to do. The herbs on the counter withering.

THE DEPARTMENT OF SECOND GUESSING

A body could fit a lot of things
into that mouth: almonds that have
been to the swimming pool, engineers
who design tests for dummies to
crash into. In movies, people
who sing to themselves in public
look happy and bright. In life,
we cannot stand up to see them.
I am thinking about the first man
who taught me to make a steak
and how he will die in his bed.

The Anxiety Werewolf

Pineapple heart, you're a
jarful of bees.

A quiet stadium.

Ice is desperation—it
used to be harvested.
Now we
make it.

Places to sit become fewer
and far so I'm hiding
in a bathroom across
the city while you're
actually shitting at home.

Guava tongue, you're a
lungful of butter.

We make new rhythms on
Pompeii instruments but
the strings
are breaking.

You write a note I read
backwards, but spoken aloud it's
upside down & transcribing
makes it right again.

Starfruit womb, you're an
eyeful of planets.

PROMENADE ALONG ALLÉE OF HONEY LOCUSTS

Think of moving

walkways. This moment
sequential

to the previous one, trees

clipping this moment and
the next and each

that comes after

and after. We drift
like solutes

across the membrane

trunks form. The planner
did not seek

plant transcendence: plate

of soil impermeable
to sky. Typology proliferates

like a syllable. So does genetic code.

Know we too are

permutations of other.

An aching sameness.

As if we tore
all the shifting

wild from the wood.

J.R. TORISEVA, *WINNER OF THE PATRICIA*
GOEDICKE PRIZE IN POETRY

LIBRARY OF SOUND

Velvet books, dropped in water, float up, ink held.
The pond grows greener every day, algaed surface, on gravel

the bindweed closes in over the arch. Tlitlizin, so far north, I should be
dream walking instead of swimming, so I stay awake at the edge.

Iliad, the journey round the pond. Iliad
underground. Iliad underneath. Ulysses in utero.

The babies always came in system. It is the looped sistus.
Wyrd's volcanic cauldron, Freyja's oaken keep.

What is held in space, in water? What keeps us
checked in: in time, in line, in rhythm?

Checked out of Dante's purgatory. Clocked in Dante's heaven.
Hell bled out in the field overlays, caught in the swath

of hay, the cut of wheat, the sheaves over the ditch, the gravel strewn with silage,
in the phosphorous scent of summer, the words become water,

shrouding me with symbols, caressing me with lines.
I sleep in syllable. I lie in rhyme.

At Table, Blank Wedding

The serving set for seven, minus butter knife
and salt cellar. This is the tile I burned. This
the plate I ran red ochre and yellow paste across,

over and over, in time for dinner.
The tablet set. The supper on.
The purple skins of the egg

plant charring the borage;
a vinaigrette of fugue and tears.
The phone at my ear, the voice

a lie in my blood stream,
but our hearts pump together
in stillness. Unannounced, The thief, the

calculator and the Roman steps. Untracked,
the train late. The baggage checked.
The déjà vu ticket stamped. Ignoring

other elements, I eat pond. I travel through.
We board, over and over, overboard and under
the dock, under board, and overturned.

The ceremony set for eleven; the wedding conducted
in darkness: night the consecrator, night the witness, night
the feasting, night the guest, night unsettling, night the ring

Syllable

Unseated, the pond is the place to rest,
a place to hole up, a way in, a place

to hold out, a way out, a place
to remember that other life form,

a place to float outside of the migratory
self. It is the gift of water.

It is the gift of deep,
though not ocean, nor sea monster.

I set my cubed self against the cat tail.
I walk a horseshoe, rest an oval

as deep as ferns,
as bottomless as high grass.

Here is the envelope of water.
Here is the signet, the fold and the stamp.

This pond fits the letter.
This pond fastens the seal.

Here I send self to self, keeping
the lines light in my hand; I sight the serpent,

seeing the stories shed, watching the end
bite the beginning, hereafter to heretofore,

furthermore to evermore, amazement to amazement,
tooth to nipple, claw to lip, and later, the again to the again.

S. K. STRINGER

SAVIORS OF LONELINESS

This is a work nonfiction. Some names have been changed in order to protect identity.

My apartment in Baku, Azerbaijan was romantic until the cats arrived. Though small, my room opened up to the balcony with a front-row view of one of the only two Orthodox churches, its silver-plated onion dome topped with a cross and surrounded by a felt green roof, and further in the distance were beige minarets capped in gold of a new mosque. Certain mornings, mesmerized, I stood at the edge of the balcony and watched religious ceremonies performed outside of the church, just yards from my apartment, where women covered in headscarves and men in religious robes prayed and sang. A priest swung a thurible in the air in the metered rhythm of a metronome from which incense flowed, its smoky scent reaching me on typical windy days.

At first, the apartment was a sanctuary, a reprieve from the city's culture shock, the car horns that never stopped but only lessened late at night, the men who dominated the streets after sundown, gathering in teahouses, wearing only black or gray, and the staring eyes of both men and women, not because I was a foreigner. I blended in easily enough, until I opened my mouth. I have dark brown hair, blue eyes, and mild olive skin. Generally, Azerbaijanis have thick black hair, are short in stature, with medium-toned skin. Azerbaijanis stare, both men and women, at everyone. My body language only helped me to stand out. In my twenties I'd been a dancer, and I was not skilled at standing still. When I wanted to fit in, and at times I did, we all want to be anonymous, I restricted my own movement, that desire to stretch, an exercise in itself to deny the impulses of what would be deemed here as grand gesture.

Those first two months, September and October of 2012, I was constantly stimulated by newness. I took photographs. Walking to my neighborhood metro station Nizami my first time, nothing was ordinary. In front of a dilapidated wall was tendir, oval-shaped Azeri bread strapped to a three-legged chair with rope as advertisement like a passenger buckled up before flight. A middle-aged woman wearing a headscarf sold lemons out of a cart. I bought two lemons, tucked them into my purse, and walked into the metro where people physically pushed in front of the ticket booth. One man tried to cut. I yelled at him: *Pujalusta, budte terpliviy* (Please, be patient). He was frustrated by my slowness, gesturing at me while speaking in Azerbaijani. My irritation burned off easily. These very annoyances were the cultural differences I sought, and newness trumped any negative feelings, usually. The escalator's descent was so long that I couldn't spot the train platform below, and across from me, where the escalator ascended, the heads, torsos, and legs of passengers lifted into view in a habitual cadence that surprised me nonetheless for I didn't know whom to expect. On the platform, I held my camera up to a tile mosaic but before my finger reached the button, a guard yelled at me. Photos, I was told, were prohibited after terrorist attacks in '94. I'd read about the attack but forgot. In that moment, more than other social blunders, I was obviously the tourist, the foreigner, able to forget a traumatic event because it hadn't happened to me on American soil. During rush hour, people pressed and pushed so forcefully to both enter and exit that I felt as though my feet weren't even on the ground. Weightlessly, I entered the train for the first time.

This stimulation was great distraction from my personal woes. My husband Steven was in America at his new job as assistant professor in northern California. He would have come, he'd said, if he hadn't found work. Though I'd wanted to live overseas, I was anxious about having oceans separating us again. In 2008, he'd lived for six months in Russia while I lived in the States during the first year of my MFA program in creative writing. We were making decisions based on our academic careers, and these very decisions were separating us.

"Who turns down a Fulbright?" he'd asked.

I'd considered it, and for the record, people turned down all sorts of things. But at the time, and I would be absolutely wrong about this, I'd thought that going alone overseas to Azerbaijan was my last long-term trip I would make without Steven, and seeing this confidently and as a smart career move, I accepted the fellowship.

"We'll be fine. We'll talk every few days on Skype," Steven had said. He promised to visit me during Christmas, which meant we'd be apart for almost four months.

In Baku, I blamed the Internet that failed us. After our Skype calls dropped the first few weeks, Steven and I resorted to chatting on Skype. When I missed his face, his six-foot body, his barrel chest and milky voice, I would call anyway just to see him. But he'd freeze on the screen and I'd become sad. Another time, and more than once, he ignored my calls and emails because he was angry with me for various reasons, one being that I had gone to a bar at night. I sympathized with his insecurities. I'd been in his shoes before when he'd been in Russia, imagining the foreign country as an alluring place for an affair, geography itself a seductress. Anywhere, though, I knew, was an easy location for an affair. And it would have been easy. Other foreigners were lonely, and some men who knew I was married hit on me anyway. I was lonely, too, and I missed having sex, but I didn't struggle with monogamy overseas or stateside. Steven tracked my patterns via Skype, seeing when I turned on my computer (which equated to Sandra returning home late), yet other times he begged for me to come back to America in a sad voice like yearning that left me feeling torn as though I now had a choice to make even though I'd already made it, with his blessing, even with him inciting such an opportunity, to live in Azerbaijan for nine months.

I had my roommate Harriet to talk to sometimes. We never became close. She is German and taught German language for four years in Baku. She didn't seem happy there and was easily frustrated, but hers was a love story in the end. She would marry an Azeri man, one of her students, who spoke her language and was headed to Germany on scholarship to study to be a doctor. They now have a child together. But before all of this, she seemed desperate to leave. Sometimes she cried in frustration because students weren't doing assignments. They came to class empty-handed. They talked and texted while she lectured. Worse, they weren't showing up. I experienced similar frustrations my first two months. I taught ESL and academic writing. I collected cell phones from the busy hands of texting fingers. By the end of a class, I might have thirteen out of thirty-two phones, but by the end of the year, I might have collected zero because they knew I'd take them. My first semester, I had unfair expectations. Some of my students were plagiarizing. As topics for their descriptive essays, some students wrote about Azerbaijani women being the most beautiful and Azerbaijan being the best country. Sometimes I wondered if I was in a version of North Korea. In America, plagiarizing was an ethical issue, also, an issue of laziness. Americans knew better, though they still cheated. To alter lessons for Azerbaijanis, I needed to understand what they'd been taught and how they'd been taught. When I surrendered to certain expectations, teaching became easier, and I taught better. This had been something in my control.

Most foreigners spoke of loneliness, what they missed back home or what issues made them feel like outsiders in Baku. One American missed her dog, another, her husband; many missed clean air and grass to lounge on. An American teacher said she missed working with school officials who were truthful; also, she missed the ability to be anonymous. In Baku, with her glorious height and her comfortable white sneakers, she stood out amid the women petite, despite their stilettos, because of their stilettos. Loneliness might have been one of the reasons Harriet rescued three feral kittens one fall day that were lying in front of our apartment building outside of a shoe store where I would linger—in the shoe store—wishing I could afford some new pair of boots in a Baku boutique on some of my lonelier days. Shopping was its own brief comfort if only for the familiarity of roles.

I was followed around the store by a sales girl during which the exterior foreign world fell away as I held a boot in my hand and considered the leather, rubbed a thumb to feel texture, and imagined myself in the walking vehicle of the socially well off as compared to the manly loafers I wore that two fashionable teenaged girls made fun of me for while riding the bus. I would finally buy boots there in early winter once they went on sale. Everything was cheaper in America.

Strays are everywhere in Baku. Cats curl up on stoops, linger near apartment doors, waiting to slyly slip into the stairwell where they beg for food. Locals prefer them outside where they guard their territory like gangs, controlling their section of the courtyard. Older "aunties" might feed them scraps, but overall, the attitude toward strays is one of mild tolerance.

Harriet didn't ask me to live with cats. Instead, she scooped up the motherless kittens and contained them in our bathroom. "Look how cute they are," she said, gingerly opening the door even though they were sequestered to the well of a bucket, their three bodies nearly inanimate except for their protruding ribs displaying life in shallow breaths. They weren't cute, exactly. They were fuzzy with dirty patches of new fur, the eyes of one glued shut by its own secretions—some infection. They were, all three of them, dying.

Harriet said she would take them to the vet. I assumed the vet would put them to sleep, that euthanizing the ill kittens might be the kindest option. She returned, though, with the kittens, medication, and a diagnosis that the kitten with the piercing cry was blind. The following day, our landlord was scheduled to visit. He would kick us out if he knew we had pets, so minutes before the landlord arrived, Harriet placed the kittens in a cardboard box with punctured holes and taped the lid. The box o' cats was stored in a cabinet on our fourth floor balcony while the landlord visited for thirty minutes. With such anxiety about their condition, I could barely focus on what the landlord was saying. He knew I spoke some Russian, so he talked to me in a fast conversational speed, at times beyond my understanding. My brain was split between translating his words and simultaneously worrying if the cats were breathing. To appease him and get him out the door, I responded a lot with, "Da, da, da." After the landlord left, Harriet and I ran through my bedroom to the balcony. Like a magician, the blind one had escaped its confines, both the box and the balcony. Harriet discovered its body splayed on our paved yard behind the apartment. She carried the kitten to the vet who put it to sleep.

The same time the cats arrived, an American friend told me about a women's shelter. An Azeri woman had recently fled her village and her husband. She had brought her son with her but had no other family locally. I asked if I could meet her, and the American gave me directions. I had no social work experience. The desire to go there was a woman's impulse and a writer's impulse, too. I accepted every invitation given to me and even invited myself to students' homes. I wanted to see Azerbaijan in both its overt glory, like the flagpole, the second tallest in the world (Damn the Tajiks for first place!), and its covert ignominy, in other words, what the presidential family preferred foreigners not see—the poverty, the forced evictions of home owners and demolitions of privately owned homes on prime real estate that the government wants for its own end.

The shelter was in a secret location, and the directions to get there by foot were like this: At the guard station turn left. Keep the flag on your right. Pass a fruit stand, etc. Those directions were housed within the fortress walls of Baku's twelfth-Century city called the Old City at the western edge of the Caspian Sea. The oil in the air was palpable—the wind wafting the scent of the country's most valuable and incendiary commodity from water to land. I walked narrow, twisting alleyways and pale cobblestone streets as I looked for the various landmarks. Just before I turned a corner to the shelter, I saw one of my students, a gregarious young woman who was walking with a man hand in hand.

"Teacher," she said, and her red-painted lips that matched her stilettos opened in surprise, "Don't tell anyone you saw me, please!"

I promised her that I wouldn't, and wondered if they walked these streets protected by the fortress only to hold hands, to be invisible to everyone but each other.

In these streets, I was reminded of the book *Ali and Nino*, a novel about an aristocratic Azerbaijani man and a Georgian princess who fall in love (Azerbaijan's *Romeo and Juliet*) set during a turbulent milieu, the early 1900s, the eve of the Bolsheviks. In the book, Ali says, "Our old town is full of secrets and mysteries, hidden nooks and little alleys."

The shelter was dilapidated with a crumbling brick exterior and narrow wooden doors so skewed that they didn't align. The neighboring building was new, its brick smooth and whole. In the background were the Flame Towers, pointed glass buildings in construction that, surrounded by so many stone buildings centuries old and a few stories tall, appeared like an exaggerated harbinger of future architecture—a glass city. This, in essence, was Baku, the old and the new rubbing up against each other in a visual story of fast wealth, historic irrelevance, and a country's effort to get notice. I couldn't imagine this neglected building as a place where women lived, a place specifically for women to feel safe, to be comforted. I knocked, no answer. I turned the knob with the assumption I'd find it locked, but it wasn't, and I entered.

Opposite the entrance was an office. At a desk were two women. The older one introduced herself in Russian as the director and the younger woman looked at me but said nothing. I told them my name and that I was the American's friend. She had told them I was coming to visit. I was about to elaborate but the director walked me ten paces to the main room and pointed to a woman named Gusel sitting on a couch who had just arrived a few days ago. For some reason, the director left us alone, and I didn't know if she trusted me because I was a woman or, perhaps, if I had a certain privilege as an American.

Gusel wore the mix-matched clothing of village women, pale blue terrycloth jogging pants with a lateral white stripe and a thick pink turtleneck sweater with gold-threaded design that covered all but the bottom of an oversized red shirt underneath.

Her face was stunning, wide brown eyes common among the men and women here, a soft jawline, a perfectly balanced face with youthful skin and a fading green bruise around her right eye. She smiled softly at me with downcast eyes. She didn't know Russian, so beyond a basic introduction in Azeri, we had to rely on gestures and a dictionary when none of the staff was around to translate. She sat in a chair while her son, a two-year-old boy with hair shaved at the sides in two-inch arcs above his ears, moved like a tornado, his hands grabbing at electrical cords, his fingers investigating a heating vent, his legs leaping onto the couch. I couldn't tell if he was showing off for me, a newcomer, or if this was routine, a little boy expending his little boy energy. Postcard-sized advertisements from a clothing store were stacked on a coffee table. I grabbed a pile of them, and the boy and I built little houses together on the floor.

At the apartment, I had little sympathy for the cats. They'd gained strength. Out of the bucket they were normal kittens, though still a bit ragged, a bit wild, with indefatigable energy. When Harriet opened her bedroom door, they ran out and attacked my feet with their claws. She allowed them to run up her body, and when she wasn't wearing pants, they left a trail of scratches and sometimes blood on her skin. Harriet didn't care. She was in love with them. I wasn't. In my animal rights concerns of my youth, I'd worked at a shelter in Clark's Summit, Pennsylvania, tangled in four dog leashes walking along State Street, and at the end of the day, I cleaned up cat and dog excrement. Some weekends, I handed out brochures with grainy black and white photographs that revealed how factory chickens were abused—stuffed into cages and force-fed drugs—all in the setting of the Viewmont Mall where my peers, who thought I was a hippie, roamed with the weight of sheer boredom with Orange Julius cups in hand. My older sister's solicitude was different and, likely to her, opposite of mine—abused children. She didn't approve of my sympathy for animals. People were further up the chain of importance; therefore, my sympathies were mistaken. Tolstoy wrote about wealthy Russian women who cried at the theater yet who were oblivious to their coachmen waiting outside for them in freezing temperatures. I was the Russian aristocrat who couldn't care for what was right in front of my face, the rescued kittens.

I walked to the shelter every other day some weeks and felt the charge of the unknown coupled with the anxiety of Gusel's fate. All I knew to do was to talk with her and to give her son attention. I didn't assume that I could solve her problems or save her. Sometimes a volunteer who spoke English and later became my friend was working at the shelter. She told me that Gusel had escaped her abusive husband and absconded with enough money only for bus fare. The husband not only physically abused her regularly, but he also had pushed her down a staircase when she was pregnant. She lost her second baby. Whenever the volunteer and I spoke, Gusel sat in a metal chair whose back cushion was held together with tape. The room was wallpapered in a lime green flower pattern. There were two couches, and both were covered with red polyester blankets. Opposite the entrance was a doorless doorway. From the threshold hung a plastic leaf room divider behind which was a set of bunk beds, the room itself small and triangular that fit nothing else. Every time I visited her she and her son were in the same clothes and she only sat in that one chair.

During the third week of the cats' stay, I came home from work and sat with my computer on my lap in bed researching and writing lesson plans. As I typed, a black bug jumped out of my keypad, then another. I reconsidered the small pink bumps that I'd noticed accumulating from the past few nights around my ankles in a linear pattern. Fleas, the kittens brought fleas, I realized. For a week, I'd been inadvertently volunteering my skin as their lifeline.

I slammed my computer shut, leaped off of the bed, stripped it, and aired my bedding on the balcony, a process I would perform numerous times, washing and air drying every piece of clothing and bedding in my room.

That night, Harriet came home from work and I ran to her.

"Look, flea bites," I said.

Harriet was very calm about the situation. She showed me her pale arms.

"They like you," she said.

My sympathy for Harriet and the cats was fading fast, a feeling untethered. Sympathy has been labeled as both misguided and misplaced. Philosopher David Hume believed that passions were irrational either when they are "founded on the supposition of the existence of objects which really do not exist or when exerting any passion in action we choose means insufficient for the designed end and deceive ourselves in our judgment of cause and effects." Harriet's passion for the kittens wasn't questionable, but I didn't believe she deliberated about which actions would be best for the cats' sake. Instead, she acted spontaneously. We want to feel like saviors, in any small way possible. We want to feel good.

The fleas had bitten up my feet, calves, hands, and the skin behind my knees, taking residence in my closet and bed. Some nights, I slept on my friend's couch, which made my husband more suspicious. In the city light of night, I believed every dark pinhead-sized ball of fuzz on the couch and blanket to be a bug. I kept slapping myself. Steven questioned where I was sleeping despite my telling him. I called him one of those nights, partly to prove where I was as well as to discuss Christmas break. He'd yet to buy his ticket. Steven had news for me.

"It's too stressful to think of coming to Baku for Christmas. I just can't do it," he said. I was surprised and I wasn't.

Already, in late fall, I was acclimating to Azerbaijani culture and had a mild fear about breaking my new rhythm here by going back home. It hadn't been our plan. I knew, though, that we needed to see each other. We fought. I told him my concerns for myself and for us, and he said he just couldn't make the trip but needed to see me. I would never know how he felt after turning off Skype that night. Perhaps satisfied or relieved. I felt defeated. I knew I was the more compromising of the two, and I also knew he wouldn't come. He'd already made up his mind.

The next morning, I returned to my apartment to get

dressed for teaching. As I lifted a glass of water from my shelf, a flea jumped into my mouth. Or did it? I screamed. I told Harriet that we had to talk. "The cats must go," I said. "I didn't ask to live with them." Her eyes teared. "I know," she said. "Give me a day," she said. The following day, she placed the kittens outside, but unlike the neighborhood cats that lived without shelter, Harriet's kittens resided in a cardboard mansion. She'd cut and shaped boxes for them against the back of the building and accessorized with our hand towels for rugs, bowls from our cabinets for drinking water, the landlord's bowls. I aired out my belongings again. Her lugubrious mood returned. The cats were gone. She made hot chocolate from one of the care packages that her mother had sent her from Germany and closed her door to the world.

The last time I saw Gusel, I was sitting with her and her son in the living room. This was my tenth visit. The boy was now comfortable enough to sit on my lap. I held his warm body and stroked his bangs across his forehead to kiss him before he jumped down to run through the room again. A male voice from the hallway filled the room like a storm cloud. Gusel stood up and sat beside me on the couch for the first time. The director entered, followed by an older woman wearing all black, her clothes magnifying the sudden change of mood. She wore a skirt to her feet, a too large leather coat that hung past her knees, and her gray hair, long and unkempt, reached her mid-back. Gusel took my hand, a gesture she'd never made before, and squeezed. She knew the woman.

"Your mother?" I whispered to her in Russian.

She understood, nodding her head. Later I would learn that the elder was her mother-in-law. The room comfortably held four people. We were nine. Women I never met before filled the room. Chairs were brought in. I wasn't told to leave, but the director wanted to sit beside Gusel, so I moved to one of the chairs across from her.

The man, Gusel's husband, entered like a celebrity, confident, and a woman gestured a place for him to sit near me. He appeared to be in his early forties. He had a handsome face, chiseled, a sprinkling of gray amid a head of thick black hair he'd gelled into a slick wave, and he called to his son, opening a bag of treats. The father lifted his boy, but the boy wiggled from his grasp, his shirt bunching up to his chest as he escaped. He grabbed the bag of candy and spread it on the floor like treasure, dividing it into dreamy categories I couldn't understand. The entire conversation was in Azerbaijani. Without looking in my purse, I felt for my camera. I brought it everywhere. I pushed the video record button, my fingers moving by memory, praying I had touched the right button as though concrete evidence had the power to change something as large as abuse. The recording would work, a colleague would translate it, and the following is an excerpt of the conversation:

Husband: "I am intelligent, but you are not smart."

Employee: "All right, Gusel. Let's assume you get divorced. What are you going to do?"

Gusel: "You can't take our son."

Husband: "Yes, I can."

Director: "The husband has the right to take the son. The government will come and see that your son is living in a shelter and will take him!"

The husband turned to me. "Who are you?" I assumed he asked something like this and I answered in Russian, saying that I was Gusel's friend.

He spoke to the director in Azeri and she told me that I had to leave.

"Gusel doesn't want me to leave," I said, but the director grabbed my arm and escorted me to the door.

The next day, I returned to the shelter with my camera, eager to have Gusel listen to the recording, but she wasn't there. When I inquired with the staff, they reported, with indifferent expressions, that she'd left. The words had barely exited their mouths before they turned their backs to me and stopped answering my questions. Though my friend no longer volunteered at the shelter, I asked her to investigate. The director told her that they didn't know where Gusel was, but she did find out that the husband had bribed the police to reveal the shelter's location. I wondered how much he had paid, how much the police believed jeopardizing a woman's safety was worth.

I checked hospitals. I returned to the shelter. Finally, after many requests and phone calls, a women's rights organization met with me. They told me the shelter had a good reputation and said they could do no more than suggest what I'd already done, look for Gusel locally. I was not permitted to have her address, assuming that she might be back home, forced to live with her abusive husband. I went to the shelter less frequently, and then,

I stopped going altogether. I don't know how to measure time spent with another. I believe Gusel felt my care for her and her son, but would my time have better served her situation if I instead worked with a women's organization versus these private visits to the shelter? My own sympathy was spontaneous and misguided. The issue was too immense, my gesture too minuscule, not capable of affecting change. I am, ultimately, attempting to measure failure.

Regardless of the fleas still hiding and jumping in my bedroom, I slept there that first week the kittens lived in their cardboard home. In the morning, I awoke to more bites and distressed messages from Harriet via text: The cats are dead! Please clean up their bodies because I can't bear to see them again after work! Calmly, I changed out of my pajamas and grabbed a handful of garbage bags, two I would use as gloves, the others for the bodies, not yet awake to the idea of handling dead animals. Harriet said the kittens were in the courtyard, but when I stood in the back of the building, I didn't see anything until I walked to the center where, barely noticeable, fresh blood puddled on the pavement, but no cats. Someone else must have picked up the corpses. I stomped on the cardboard houses and threw them away in the dumpster. Winter had arrived last week with wind gusts that howled in the narrow city streets like a lamenting voice. The sound was human, ardent. Today, the sun shone, the day seemed without wind at all, and leaning beside a wire fence was an auntie wearing a fur coat, dull and flat, likely a few decades old, her palm filled with bread crumbs from which a large gray cat, one of the bullies, ate. She spoke sweet words to him: *krasivaya koshka* (beautiful cat), *milaya koshka* (sweet cat). In Russian, I asked her if she knew anything about the kittens. She said that a lot of people in the building hate the cats. "They are dirty," she said. One man in particular complained about the new kittens and early this morning, he slit their throats and exhibited them in the center of the courtyard. The auntie, though saddened by retelling the story, for she obviously was dedicated to caring for these communal animals, also understood why the neighbor killed them. She had an acceptable role at the apartment building that other women held as well, feeding the cats outside, in their territory.

I wasn't sleeping well and felt, at times, crazy with fleabites.

"I should move out," I told my husband one night, typing the words on Skype chat.

He didn't like the idea because by moving out I would live alone, which meant I'd be spending more of my fellowship money and, in retrospect, I realized, he preferred the idea of me living with another woman. There was security for him in that. Maybe the nights my husband was most jealous of me were directly after his nights of infidelity. I can only make assumptions in hindsight. Upon returning to America, I would discover he'd been cheating, but for how long, and with how many women, I'll never know. I now imagine his disloyalty like cause and effect, like a lesson in logic or a lesson in psychology. He didn't trust me because a) he couldn't be trusted; b) he didn't know how to trust anyone; or c) he didn't trust himself. My husband held his tall stature erectly with his shoulder blades pinched together, eyes narrow in his staid expression. All the life behind someone's eyes. Or, as Ali said in the novel, "But you will never know what is hiding behind those eyes, even when you think you know her well."

A month after the cats died and Gusel and her son disappeared was Christmas. I left Baku to visit Steven, thinking I was strengthening my marriage. We binge-watched *Friday Night Lights*. We cried at times watching it, perhaps too much, too easily. He imagined, I knew, himself as the coach in the show, a local hero, a savior who swoops in to a new town and inspires undergrads to be better than they think they can be. And he did accomplish that. It was one of his strengths. He wanted to see himself as good. We made love under the Christmas tree, in the bed, on the couch, all without protection in the hopes of making a baby. We walked around our town in a snowless December and we looked at houses for sale. We walked in overgrown grass and I climbed on top of his shoulders so I could look in the windows at the empty rooms, and we named the rooms: our bedroom, his office, my office, the baby's room.

Love dies and does not. I will never have that very specific love I'd had with Steven again. Our coupling created a trajectory unfit for anyone but us. Steven was at first sweet when I returned home from Azerbaijan in July of 2012, but a thread unraveled. He started keeping his cell phone in his office. He started sleeping in the living room, getting mad at me for no reason, making it more awkward in the house considering we had a roommate, another professor. He stopped answering my calls, but more than all of the physical evidence, the truth was in his eyes. After four months home, I confronted him about the affairs, but he denied everything. He couldn't look me in the eyes, but I looked into his, and they were empty. *All the lifelessness in someone's eyes.* I packed up a few boxes. Steven remained away from the house until I left. My girlfriend picked me up the following afternoon. She drove six hours alone to fetch me. I could have taken the plane, but I didn't want to if I could help it. Packing alone that night, I'd only thought to put a few belongings in boxes. I'd forgotten I owned luggage. I hadn't thought to bring a towel or a toothbrush. I couldn't imagine sitting on a plane with strangers, sitting in that small airport with its cancellations due to fog, the lonely wait of it.

Sometimes all that you have are things, books, a coffee mug, tchotchkes, souvenirs, and the like. When I moved into a new apartment alone, I had some of my belongings in boxes that remained stacked in the center of the apartment. A stranger wouldn't have known if I was moving in or out. For months, I invited no one over. For months I barely unpacked. Loneliness is like negative space—the absence of my husband's hand on my low back or the absence of his voice, enough absence to over-whelm a person, the absence of a future together, the absence of a child. On my most desperate days, it was like waiting for a dead person to walk through the door.

     I dream of Gusel. Sometimes she appears in a nightmare

where she sits in that metal chair with its taped cushion, its legs stuck in dirt as though held by cement. Other times, she is with her child in a living room like mine. She has second and third chances, but those are just dreams and I am lucky.

CHARITY OF POTATOES

The last time I talked to my Grandma she told me a story about
the Klan who—because there weren't any Blacks in South Dakota—resorted to Catholics to harass and bully from behind white
sheets. "And in the morning, they'd come and take the potatoes."
That's how she said it, too, the poe-tay-tahs—talking like two
generations didn't separate her from Ireland, recounting how in the
parsonage of a gray-wood church they now hang seed signs from
a Swiss priest kept a store of potatoes, and after Swedish farmers
took off bed sheets and stopped being mad about Grandma's family eating their God and drinking his blood they wagon-rode to the
parsonage asking for food. "They'd come and take the potatoes."
And she repeated the expression, still impressed by the audacity of
human guile, "They'd come and take the potatoes."
    "Who'd come?" I asked. "The Klu Kluxers?"
    "Yes," she replied. "The Kluxers," like some family across
the river with a lop-eared donkey—the affable Johnsons or Simp-
sons. "I don't think they even knew what they'd joined," she added,
either the easy forgiving of nursing homes or the cautious prox-
imity one keeps from True Evil—no letting-off-the-hook-of, but
rather an ignoring-of the wire, tightening and whipping in the
kerosene lamplight, stretching from porch to thick black barn door
wide open, black as hell.
    I'd like to say the world turns by gravity, falling through
space, but I think instead it's Hunger, that's why we see miracles in
barns—and why we're best at table.
    I never talked to my grandma again. She died months later.
But I think that was the point of her charitable interpretation of
her neighbors' comingling, that in the morning, when she swung

open doors, the machine shed was just a machine shed, the hoof marks or tire-tracks were lost in the crabgrass. And the parish priest locking the cellar door, just shook his head, after putting back the potatoes onto another heap of potatoes—walls up to the earthen roof, enough to feed every hungry child or beast walking the earth, potatoes the size and density of your fist, like the tiniest of storm clouds waiting to be called on, to be boiled in the water pots of the land, cut blind, skinless, tender and clean.

    If I have a granddaughter, I'd like to leave her stories of the past. But not any lessons. Just stories, and maybe Grandma's recipe for scalloped potatoes. I think that's why we pass down recipes, to make sure those who come after us are always fed, and won't worry about whether we knew or knew not whatever it was we did to tide ourselves over between meals.

MEME

Years ago in her kitchen, my Kurdish aunt Parween taught me how to make *yaprah*, stuffed vegetables and grape leaves served hot and glistening with oil at picnics and parties in Kurdistan. First, you must hollow out the vegetables, coring the eggplants with a sharp knife and scraping the inside with a spoon. You must cut the onions to the core but not past, and coax each layer apart, like separating nesting dolls. You must gently spread the grape leaves in your open palm and spoon the aromatic filling of rice and meat and dill, which you fold in tightly, so none escapes. You stack the stuffed leaves like tiny parcels in a big tin pot with an upside down plate in the bottom to keep the *yaprah* from burning while cooking over a low flame. The rice will expand, so you must know how to fill the vegetables with just enough: too little, and the vegetables will collapse as they steam. Too much, and the filling will spill out.

[]

Deep in the basement of my childhood home, there is a bookshelf filled with yellow-spined issues of National Geographic. In one of them, more worn than the rest, my grandfather is quoted, having fled his family – my family – during a Kurdish rebellion, living for three months in a cave near the Iran-Iraq border. Alongside his long-ago highlighted words are pictures of Kurdish people, who look like all the brown-skinned people in its pages, squinting into the camera.

One of the first things my father told me when I came out to him was that I didn't need to tell my grandfather, ever. He comes from a different culture, he explained, and it's true, he does.

But he comes from a country that doesn't exist. Despite the efforts of my grandfather and millions of others dreaming of a homeland, the Kurds are the largest nationless nation in the world.

[]

The same year the twin towers fall, my family takes a vacation to Spain, where we visit Alhambra, the Moorish palace in Granada. I am entranced by the intricate patterns carved into the marble, which I do not recognize as language until my father points where I am looking and begins to read. *Allahu akbar*, he says, *God is great.*

Fifteen years later, ISIS affiliates will notoriously shout this same phrase– *Allahu akbar* – before they pick off diners at a café in Paris with machine guns.

[]

The word *barbaric* comes from the Greek. In ancient times they called the Persians *barbarous* for the way they sounded when they spoke, making sounds like a babbling brook. What was foreign was seen as savage, as uncivilized.

It is easy to recognize what is barbaric. Humans who don't seem human repulse us.

[]

Last spring, CNN reported on an alleged ISIS flag among the rainbow crowds of London's Pride Parade. But its lettering was made from the shapes of dildos and butt plugs, cut from white cloth and stitched to the banner.

The flag was not a prank, but the work of an artist, in protest of the Islamic State, which even Al-Qaeda has dismissed as excessive in its cruelty.

Like Kurdistan, ISIS is a construct. It spreads it dark stain over the map where I locate homeland. But there are people for whom it is the answer.

On CNN the reporters go on oblivious. They acknowledge only that the script does not quite appear to be Arabic, reporting, instead, that it looks like "gobbledygook."

[]

Despite two years of formal study, I cannot carry on a conversation in Arabic. I can read the script without comprehending anything but the few words I do know, which rise out of the texts like little islands. After reading reports of a woman my age recruited by ISIS on Twitter, I spend hours scrolling through pages of tweets in Arabic, which I cannot read, cannot comprehend. I detect in myself all the hallmark signs of fear: my heart quickens; my chest clenches; my body floods with heat.

The unknown is frightening because we cannot see it, cannot touch it. It is like walking into a dark cave. You do not know what dangers threaten you, and dangers may be unrecognized as such. Our senses are hindered at best and useless at worst.

[]

While waiting in the doctor's office in Brooklyn, I watch two women kiss on the TV. *WHAT*, whispers one little girl beside me to the other. *GAY*, the other whispers back, eyes squinched with disgust.

[]

I am in the US capitol with my girlfriend when my future wedding is legalized by nine strangers. *Congratulations*, says a woman on the street. *Are you planning on getting married now?* I smiled, but later, feel this was invasive.

That afternoon, *Foreign Policy* publishes an article titled, "Can Gay Marriage Defeat the Islamic State?" It suggests that we fight terrorism by posting and tweeting pictures of gay people kissing. It is very stupid.

By then I have already uploaded a photo of my girlfriend and I kissing on the steps of the Supreme Court, a rainbow flag behind us.

By then ISIS has already posted a video of four allegedly gay men being flung from a rooftop and stoned when they hit the street.

[]

Among the flurry of media flooding the internet after the marriage equality ruling, I see a video produced by a friend for the Kurdish news.

Two minutes in, I recognize myself in the background, unmistakable in a black cap and floral button up, kissing my girlfriend.

My heart pounds until the clip ends without my figure ever coming into focus. But undoubtedly, dozens of my relatives watched me without knowing as the footage played and replayed in their living rooms in Kurdistan while they sucked their teeth with disapproval.

[]

It wasn't the first time I'd felt so publicly invisible. After my first summer in Kurdistan, I received a barrage of messages from relatives alerting me of a photo being passed around on Facebook. I recognize it: it's me in a yellow dress, shaking hands with the then-president of Iraq, but my face is swapped out for the face of a man with a mustache.

My cousin explains: it's a political joke, mocking the president, but I can't make any sense of it. I'm stuck on the fact that I'd been made into a meme.

[]

Like the word barbaric, the word meme also comes from Greek, adapted from the word *mimema*, or "imitated thing." A meme spreads within a culture: it's an idea, a behavior or style, passed from person to person in the viral manner of a disease. Mimetics can explain the spread of radical Islamic ideology, and also the rapid acceptance of gay rights in the United States.

[]

The family in Kurdistan reacts to photo I posted of me kissing my girlfriend. *Change your profile picture*, writes one cousin. *I really hate this rainbow flag*, she says, *since I learned what it means.*

A former American student of mine in New York City finds the photo and shares it on Facebook. "Fagot ass hoe," [sic] comments one of her classmates. "I didn't no she went the other way," [sic] writes another. Twenty-four more of them comment with sad faces, crying faces, and acronyms I can't make sense of.

I wasn't scared to post the picture, but I'm scared to take it down. I'm scared of breaking down, of caving in. But eventually, I do. Eventually I take it off Facebook altogether. Eventually I want it to disappear. I delete it from where it once appeared in this essay.

[]

My grandfather emails the family, everyone but me. He invites everyone to come back to Kurdistan and praises what fine young men my brothers have become, but I remain unmentioned.

I feel as if I've made some trade without intending to, putting Kurdistan on the chopping block while I reveled in some paltry rainbow victory. I'm flattened by forces much bigger than I am.

My father insists I'm being paranoid.

I think of the time a student wrote DYKE on my whiteboard, and his mother insisted he couldn't have known what the word meant, that it was a just a coincidence. The principal seemed to believe this, and at the time, I almost did, too.

[]

Traditional Kurdish clothes for women consist of a sheer gown with long, trailing sleeves that are tied in the back, worn over modest undergarments and topped with a colorful overdress, embroidered with so many beads and sequins that it sits heavier than a winter coat.

The effect is stunning, but immobilizing.

[]

According to legend, the Kurdish people arose when 400 women were banished from the Persian Empire and sent to die in the mountains. But instead of disappearing, they were raped by devils, and the children they gave birth to became the Kurds. Some say that the Kurds are cursed.

[]

Currently, there are more than 2,000 Kurdish and Yezidi women held by ISIS as sex slaves, although no one knows the true number.

In the videos of women and girls who've escaped, they blur out the victims' faces to protect them, so that they appear as their captors saw them: faceless, erased. In Kurdistan, it is so shameful to be raped that some fathers choose to kill their daughters rather than live with the dishonor.

[]

According to family legend, and the menu of my Auntie's Kurdish restaurant in St. Paul, my grandfather arrived in Minnesota after hearing a radio broadcast exalting the state's strong, blonde, and beautiful women.

As it is written:

> "The great leaders of this mighty empire could not contain the curiosity of young men, whose desires to explore the treasures of exotic lands were insatiable.
> In keeping with their Babani male tradition, this especially applied to the wonders of women."

Even my own family attributes my grandfather's arrival in America to sexual appetite, to lust.

[]

It would be easy to believe the Kurds are cursed. When ISIS razes a village, it's destroying homes rebuilt from rubble. The bombshells from Saddam's genocidal campaign against the Kurds still sit in the streets of Halabja, where 5,000 Kurds were gassed the year before I was born. People still limp on legs where shrapnel entered their flesh. Babies are still born deformed.

Deformed. Consider the word. Consider the prefix *de-*, which signifies removal, separation, negation.

At a certain level of suffering, it becomes difficult or impossible to access the self.

[]

In English we describe emotional pain with a vocabulary of fracture and the resulting pieces.

He fell apart. I suffered a breakdown. The experience left her shattered.

Being "in pieces" is synonymous with being broken.

And perhaps, in a place as thoroughly shattered as Kurdistan, so broken it doesn't exist, it's hard to see someone made of parts, of multiple identities, as anything but broken.

[]

Or at least, this is a common justification for lagging LGBT rights in the parts of the world where privation and violence are common. *We will worry about gay rights when everyone has access to water and food,* they say. *We have more important things to deal with at the moment.*

It's tempting to yield to this. I harbor guilt.

But all of these pieces have grooves that fit together. ISIS espouses an ideology that persecutes anyone who doesn't conform. Rape as a weapon of war is most effective in a culture where shame flourishes. Some go as far to as to speculate ISIS is effective in recruiting new members because of the promise of sex among the sexually oppressed.

[]

"The oppressed, instead of striving for liberation, tend themselves to become oppressors." -- Paulo Freire, *Pedagogy of the Oppressed*, 1968.

[]

The summer I taught English in my grandfather's village, my students used to take me berry picking after class. One afternoon I snapped a photo of our open palms, stained vivid red. Later, when the photo was displayed in a gallery in Chicago, everyone assumed the berry juice was blood.

[]

I have felt so many times that there is no room for me to be Queer and Kurdish. To be Kurdish is to have survived genocide. There is no room for rebellion against cultural norms when your culture itself is under attack. But to deny who you are is to attack yourself.

[]

For two years I had no contact with my grandfather. I thought of him in his vineyard, the dry brown hills, his puffed up pride at his orchard of stone fruits and fields of parched watermelon plants. I thought of him in that cave, and all the metaphors that go with it – being in the dark, leaving your family for something you believe in.

My father asked me why I'd been banished. I shrugged, feigning disinterest, too ashamed to tell him I think I'm unwelcome there because of who I am.

The two summers I lived with my grandfather in Kurdistan, we'd open a bottle of his wine every night. The wine, made from grapes stomped in a big plastic bucket, was bitter and silty, but I'd always tell my grandfather it was delicious, and it was. It tasted how I imagined it would taste to drink the earth.

[]

I'm desperate to claim my Kurdish identity. It's as if the iron in my blood has been magnetized to pull me to my homeland. It's the endless cups of tea in tiny glass cups that burn your fingers, the way my aunt says *yallah* when it's time to go; the picnics by the highwayside and Kurdish music pumped out the speakers of someone's car. One day, I will return. It's not that it's perfect – it's a place filled with landmines, real and metaphoric. Like so many things, I love it because it is mine. I belong to it; it belongs to me; and that is enough.

REAL CALIFORNIA LIVING

It is while you are showing me the shelving in the garage that I understand you and your husband have lost a child. The two of you are standing below a cardboard box with thick black letters on its side, *Winter, 18-24 months*, and one of you has drawn a heart below the words. The heart gives you away, and the box of diapers and the box for a baby walker, all above your head on the shelf as you try to sell me your house.

"Nice big space out here. You could have a little craft station, there's enough room," my husband Sam says into my ear as you and your husband watch us, pretending not to listen, wondering if our Lexus in your driveway means we have the money to buy your house. I don't know why my husband thinks I want a craft station; I don't do crafts. Why is it that the idea of a new house seems to invite the idea of a new life entirely? When I see the box, I put it together with the bare third bedroom you said you'd painted brand-new, the plastic plugs in all the outlets, the way you are not filling out your jeans. It's like one of those photographs made up of other tiny photographs. "We're moving to Colorado, a small condo, fresh start," you told us. Why didn't you throw away the boxes? Your husband had made a point to say it was just the two of you. I wonder now how the words felt in his mouth, if someone had advised him to do this, for closure.

The house is very nice, ranch-style like no one ever has as a dollhouse, a house that really says California to people like me who live here now but always feel like they're just visiting. There is a courtyard where you've put metal sculptures of fish, coppery with sharp edges. I've always liked this part of the valley that doesn't feel like the valley, up the mountain side of the freeway, high enough to see the Santa Anas sweep through, high enough to see the earth move in ripples if there was a five pointer, if you were lucky enough to be standing outside when it happened. You've priced it too low, and I was suspicious from the outset. Sam even told me, "They're in a hurry to leave!" but of course he couldn't have known about what had happened to you, and he still doesn't understand, even when it is all so very obvious to me.

Your husband says, "Lots of storage space, and we put in these shelves from Costco, you can store your golf clubs and your Christmas decorations and dishes in there," and he is attractive in the way that his dark blue shirt makes him look tan and he assumes we play golf and have accumulated seasonal décor, maybe even wedding china. I like him because he has married you. It says something that he chose a woman like you, a woman who wears her hair in two loose braids, who runs her hand along her books as she walks by the bookshelf. You probably did everything all natural when you birthed your child, skipped the epidural, felt it all, every twinge and every kick and every move down and out. I want to hug you in the garage. I know you would smell like jasmine. You would hug me back with both arms.

I wouldn't call you orphans, that's not the word, but surely there is a word for this? There must be at the very least a poem. I look at you both, standing under your child's tiny gloves and knit hats and other winter things 18-24 months.

"We want to move into a neighborhood just like this," Sam says to you, breaking all the rules we agreed upon before we went in: no personal details, no seeming desperate for the house. If he wanted to exclaim over granite countertops and the red tile patio, do it in the car so you wouldn't know not to accept our low offer. It's not that I want to cheat you, it's just that this is all a game. That's why they call it house hunting, but I'm no predator.

Sam says, "Fenced-in yards and a potting shed out in back? We love to garden. We could put some tomato plants in there, maybe some strawberries or zucchini."

In our eight months of marriage, Sam has never before mentioned gardening. Sure, there aren't many opportunities at the rental house, which doesn't have a yard so much as a patio and steep slopes down off the sides. There's only that strange iceplant, with the thick leaves full of watery insides, the kind on all the slopes. I don't know if my husband is trying to impress you with the gardening. He might be, but it isn't sexual. He needs to be liked. You have covered up your acne below your cheekbones with thick makeup, and it looks purple still, like a bruise. I wonder if you take off the makeup at night before you go to bed, if you wait until the lights are dim, if your husband sees you without it. I bet your husband doesn't care you have acne. I bet he tells you you're beautiful and pulls on your braids with his fingers.

Which one of you drew the heart on the box? It seems like something a mother would do, but then again, your husband has not stopped touching you.

When we move into the kitchen, Sam talks about putting a motorcycle in the extra space in the garage. Even fix one up in there, like a workshop, there's enough room, don't you think? He could get tools. He is a chameleon, and we will look at houses until he settles on a skin.

We found your house on one of those websites. You even had a slogan: "Real California Living." You had taken so many pictures, and I noticed everything was free of clutter, and you had put out clear glass vases filled with seashells to suggest the beach, even though we both know it's a solid forty-five minute drive from the house. But there were palm trees shedding their hair onto the sod, bougainvillea climbing the wooden fences, and that view, today complete with some brown gauzy air people used to call smog but now simply refer to as *haze*. The pictures of the backyard showed slopes behind the house, but unlike our rental house these slopes went up, rising into the canyons made of rocks, sitting diagonally like the fall of a slide, like the angle of a roof, so sharp I could finally understand how the earth could be twisted. Images of your house, rough stucco walls, birch trees with flaking skin, made up a California as real as all the Californias I have ever known living here and not living here. I leaned over Sam as we looked at the website, and his breath had smelled of fast food, and for the first time in my life, I was repulsed by him. It was like cutting yourself while shaving your legs, how in that moment you realize what you're holding is a knife, so close to your veins, and you think to yourself, this could cut me open.

"And how many square feet is the backyard?" Sam asks, and I wonder if he'd even know how many square feet a regular room would be. Square feet is only a thing when you're looking at houses, at no other time does the subject come up. "And the utilities? Pretty expensive?" No more than the usual cost, you assure him, and when you smile I notice your teeth are white and straight. You are beautiful when you smile, though it cracks your makeup.

I don't want to know what happened to your baby. It could have been anything, an accident, cancer. My sister miscarried at twelve weeks, and she told me after it happened she still found herself putting her hand on her stomach, in that different way she said a woman does when she's pregnant, as if her hand had a mind of its own and nobody had told it what happened. Your whole house like that hand.

Sam is telling you his life story. "My dad grew up water skiing in Long Beach," he says, "and here's a great story for you. So he's skiing one day and he sees his brother and dad waving frantically from the boat, telling him to look behind him, right? And he turns around and there's a goddamn killer whale! Right there behind him and he knew he couldn't fall, and that only makes it harder to stay up. We never really believed him, but he swears up and down that it was something big, and my uncle said the fin was really tall, too tall to be anything else, and shiny. My uncle's not the kind to lie, he was in Vietnam." You are engaged by Sam, everyone is. Even in this house where your child has died, you love his killer whale story like everyone else loves it. "You know we could put a boat in that third slot in the garage," he finishes, and he is trying on your house and this time it looks like tanned skin and smells like coconut, and I see him like his father in the photograph in our rental house, the sun on the ocean so bright behind him his face is shaded and he could be anybody.

I have no burning passions. None like Sam's, passions for Religious Studies and Communications and Film Studies and back to Religious Studies and Professional Writing and, now, History. He can teach. He has a passion for educating teenagers. He can help them get into college and decide who they want to be. I open money market accounts, I count out soft money holding all the worst smells in the world, clip a tag with his last name on it to my collared shirt. I chose it all. At no time did I say no.

I only need one thing from your house, and it is all distance, miles and minutes like the inky gape of space, the way I can see your house on a map with inches made of forgetting.

"Are there wood floors under here?" Sam points at your carpet in the living room with his toe. We have moved in there to examine, as Sam has put it, the common living space.

"No, just the carpet," you say, and Sam makes a clicking noise as if encouraging a horse.

"The house was built in the 80s, Sam," I say to defend you. You and your husband don't seem to recognize that this is what I am doing. "And I like carpet in the living room, it makes you want to walk around in bare feet."

You and your husband look at each other, and I realize maybe you thought carpet a better choice for your small baby, who would of course need a cushion while learning to crawl and walk. How dare you set me up to say something so careless. Why haven't you said anything? How cruel to leave out the box in the garage, to surprise me with your secret. I read somewhere that sellers are required to inform prospective buyers if a crime has occurred on the property. There should be full disclosure of all calamities occurring within the walls of any given house for sale. They should be stated on the website. Check all that apply: Depression, Affair, Abuse, Lies, Bitterness, Regret, Disease, Loss, Pain, Divorce. For Sale: Three Bedroom, Two Bath, Large Yard, Real California Living. Child now deceased crawled on carpeted floors in Main-Level Common Living Space.

I look at your face as you examine the room with us like it's a stranger to you, and I can't help it, I have to know, so I say, "Why are you selling your house?" I don't mean it to sting, it's just a question, but I know you don't approve. You look at me like I am a criminal, like I have smashed all your tiny bud vases on the original tile floors, stabbed you with your pointy copper fish. You say, "Colorado is beautiful. We thought it might be a place to go." It's the right answer, and your husband moves to put his whole hand around just one of your fingers. Sam misses all of this. He is back in the kitchen, open to the living room as you promised it would be, and he is poking at the grout in the tile.

"Honey, what do you think?" Sam is showing all his teeth with his smile. You look at him with surprise, then over to me. I picture your husband fallen on a hospital floor, his eyes and mouth open in grieving against the hard cold tiles, open to the blood and the spit and the dirt and the sick because he does not care, he does not know anything but this floor.

"I'm just not sure," I say, and you and your husband breathe out your disappointment at the same time, and Sam's mouth tips down at the edges.

"Of course you're not sure, you need time to think about it and everything," your husband says, and I feel another rush of affection for him, and I even wish for a moment that he is my husband. I look at his red mouth and imagine him kissing my neck, touching me softly and lingering on the small scar I have on my shoulder from when I scraped it on the bottom of a pool while diving. He would have pleasant breath, like wine or warm rolls. I imagine grieving a child with him, holding him as he cries in that silent way where tears come down hard, but he is grabbing my hair, or clutching at my stomach, maybe even cutting me with his nails. "Please," he'd cry, or "No." It would hurt, his outpouring of sorrow, but it wouldn't matter.

"Thank you," I say, and I want to climb the slopes and lie diagonally with the rocks, headfirst so I can feel the blood coming down in a hot rush behind my eyes.

"We'll be giving you a call," says Sam, with a tone in his voice that says he will convince me, he has your back on this whole thing, I'll come around, you'll see. "The guest bedroom would be perfect, you know—" he starts to say, and I interrupt him to ask you to show me the master closet one more time before we leave.

You and I go in alone. Your closet is organized, and I notice your clothes are mostly made of cotton, and you have hung even your T-shirts. Your husband's clothing takes up less room, and his shirts are ironed, and he has a collection of T-shirt jerseys with team logos on the front and last names of famous players on the back, and I wonder why it is that sports allow some men to wear costumes all their lives. You laugh and don't apologize for the mess or for the lighting, and you move quickly to shove your husband's underwear into a drawer. You have one nightgown hanging up, purple silk with pink lace on the bottom. I tried lingerie a few times with Sam, and he never once looked at it, just took it off of me very quickly, but isn't that the point?

"There used to be a hole in the ceiling in here," you say, looking up. "We didn't fix it for three years, then last week, we got it fixed. It took a half hour." You look at the clean and vacuumed carpet and you say, "It's never been this neat in here." You leave the closet before I do, before you can see me touch the nightgown as I walk by, the lace catching on my nail, and I take a thread of it with me in my palm.

"You're not going to buy this house, are you?" you say, turning around to look at me.

I am backed into your closet, under your intact ceiling.

"Just tell me." Your eyes are perfectly visible in the glow of the lightbulb, but they might as well be closed. I consider telling you, yes, I will buy it. I consider telling you what we both know about this house. I consider the idea of Real Living, anywhere.

"No, we're not going to buy it," I apologize. As we walk out, you touch your hand to a certain spot on the wall in a way that lets me know there was something there before.

There are more minutes in the house, and you leave us alone to look around by ourselves, and I follow Sam as he reminds me how long we've been looking, how he needs an office like this to finally write his memoir. He likes the color you have painted the baby's old room, but the rusty brown makes me think of dry leaves. You have disappeared somewhere, and I am listening for your footsteps.

I don't turn around as Sam and I walk down the driveway

to the car, but I imagine you've returned to your husband at the door to watch us go, and the two of you are holding hands, and maybe he is undoing one of your braids.

Sam asks me if I think I have been a bit rude as he buckles into the passenger seat. I always drive when we're together, it's well known Sam is a terrible driver. He is a tall man, and his belly has grown paunchier over these months, hanging just a bit over the lap belt, his hair hanging just a bit over his ears. As I look at him, I try very hard to see him with the urgent love I remember now only as a dream.

"How could you not know?" I say. "They lost a baby. Their baby is dead." I want to say it again. "Their baby is dead. Maybe it was an accident. There was a box with clothing sizes with a heart drawn on it. Just the two of them going to Colorado. And you almost said the guest room would be perfect for a baby!"

"Jesus," says Sam after a moment. I feel him look at me. "No, there's no way. They would have said." He does not say this like a question. In a way, it's not surprising he doesn't believe me. But I know you lost a baby like I know the alphabet. "You're always inventing things," he says into the glove box as he digs for something. "You're so creative. You should try writing poetry sometime. I'm thinking of taking a class." He emerges from the glove box with nothing and leans back into his seat, closing his eyes.

He reaches over to hold my hand and I want him to take only one of my fingers. There is no word opposite of orphan. Orphans are something to think about. There are endless stories of orphans and they are all heroes. They have novels and gangs of other orphans and surrogate parents. Disney has made a fortune on them, the orphaning the essential ingredient for bittersweet. There is no story for parents who have lost a child, only canyons, emptied skies, Rocky Mountains reaching up like blades.

I pull my hand from his and place it on the wheel. We will look at another house, and another, and we will evaluate palm trees and square feet and school districts, and we will buy a house with an open floor plan and a skylight in the master bedroom and imprints of fallen leaves in the concrete sidewalk. I will get pregnant and watch Sam hold the baby in his arms, and he will say, "Remember when we looked at that house ..." and he won't finish, because of course we both will know I remember your house, and even though we never bought it, I'll live there just the same.

BLOODLINES

THE HUSBAND

This is what it is to be married to a Romanian: on Christmas Day, my mother-in-law takes an old videocassette from the cupboard beneath her wood-paneled television set. We gather in the living room and she slides it into the VCR. Ah, I think, home movies, my wife and her sister when they were children.

No. Two white lines waver in the center of the grainy footage; it has been watched so many times. Nicolae Ceaușescu looking dazed in a black winter coat and gray fur hat; his wife Elena babbling ceaselessly in a long fur coat and yellow scarf, her graying hair escaping from a bun. Young soldiers tie their hands. They are led from the classroom where the trial was held to a courtyard. The camera shakes. They stand beside each other against a yellow concrete wall.

When Elena begins to beg for her life, my mother-in-law raises her index finger and shakes it at the screen. "Listen to her," she says. "Listen to her now. Not once did she give mercy when the people were dying in the streets."

The Ceaușescus asked to die together. They also asked for their hands to remain free. My nephew squirms in his mother's lap. Nicolae looks directly into the camera. Elena continues to beg, struggling against her bound wrists. The soldiers are off-screen, invisible. "Shame," Elena says, suddenly. "Shame on you. I raised you as a mother."

The soldiers respond with a volley of machine gun fire. The bullets knock the President and his wife back, shaking and twisting their bodies before dropping them to the ground.

Nicolae and Elena lie angled together through a haze of smoke. Their arms are pinned behind them. Their heads nearly touch. The yellow scarf and the yellow wall. A trail of blood on the flagstones.

The two white lines linger on the screen after the image has gone. "That woman," my mother-in-law says, shaking her head. "She said she was our mother."

THE MOTHER

A woman was stoned to death yesterday, halfway around the world. I hate to think about it. But we must, mustn't we? Open the paper, the magazine, suffer a bit over our morning coffee.

"I killed my daughter." This was how the father's statement began, and thinking of my own, I had trouble reading on. "I killed my daughter because she insulted our family. I have no regret."

Briefly, I considered regret. How it comes later. How it grows like a tumor in your heart.

A picture of the father accompanied the article: his stringy body pitched toward the camera, mouth open, blood on the sleeve of his robe. Looking at his face, I wanted nothing so much as to hit it with a rock. Cave in his cheek. Watch him go to his knees. The urge seized me so powerfully that I looked around my kitchen, saw the cast-iron frying pan hanging above the stove, and thought *that will do.*

I saw myself seizing the handle, lifting the pan above my head, and hurling it down end-over-end. But my aim is not so good—my son will tell you that—and the harder I throw the worse it gets. What if I missed? Would I pick up the pan and try again?

The father would try to avoid the pan as his daughter tried to avoid the stones. Ducking and twisting her body. Holding her arms in front of her eyes, choking on blood. Feeling parts of herself go numb while other parts came alive with pain. How long was she awake? Did the men—her brothers and uncles and cousins—have to go and gather more rocks? Did she watch them? Did she try to crawl away?

Oatmeal was heating on the stove but I couldn't eat. My husband came into the kitchen. He looked at me, then at the article. He kissed the top of my head, poured himself a cup of coffee, and walked out onto the deck. Men! I work in a hospital; I know how long a human body can function in shock. How strong the will to live can be. I've seen children…. No. I'd have to pick up the pan many, many times. My arm would grow sore. I'd forget who the father was, where he came from, what I was doing.

I'd rather see him shot. On television or from a great distance. Quickly, without a word. Neat and contained and in the right order of things, his body dropping like a windless sail.

THE SON

When I was still in the army, at the beginning of the second conflict, after the statues had fallen but before the city was burned, we patrolled each morning from the perimeter of our barracks to the village of F—, and each morning we encountered the worst sniper in history.

Certainly there have been others who never hit anything, but did they discharge as much ammunition, did they cause the opposing army as much comfort? I think not.

His shots pinged off the corrugated roof of the four-story warehouse across from the chemical plant where he was stationed, so high above us that we had to strain our eyes. And endless, a fusillade, like he was hunting a skein of geese except there were no birds in that country, nothing alive except what could burrow into the sand.

The high, wild trajectory of his bullets reminded us of home. We searched the sun-struck broken windows for his face. Some men waved, others raised their middle fingers. We called the factory The Banana Factory and him The Man on the Moon.

One day we stopped. Got out and stood in the sun cursing and shouting and using the few snatches of K— we'd learned in training. The dust settling from the tires whitened our faces. We kicked rocks and called each other names. We were young; everything was a test. In response, he fired a single shot into the tank's open turret hatch, threading a hole through the bottom of the periscope.

We froze like trees in the sand. As if, idiotically, this would make us more difficult targets. The ticking of the cooling engines was the only sound. Sweat burned our eyes. Then in a clanking herd, we rushed back to the tank and Humvees and clambered inside.

The rest of the day we rode in silence. Wondering what mistake we'd made, how our lives had brought us here.

The sniper continued firing over our heads for the next

month, and then one day he was gone. Vanished, like a ghost, and when we told the new recruits his story they narrowed their eyes as if he'd never been there at all. We whispered among ourselves. Had he gone home to his wife and children? Had his commanders discovered his errant shooting and piled his body among many others unclaimed in a ditch? Or had he simply moved on to sing his artillery song on another battlefield—in Syria, Egypt, or down on the shores of Lac Tchad?

A new and deeper silence fell over the village of F—. We patrolled with a sickly fear, hardly daring to whisper, the faces of our families flickering through our minds. Mother. Father. Sister. The worst. The best. In war, they were so often the same.

THE DAUGHTER

A ten-year-old girl was put back together in a crowded market today. Security officers were surprised to find her standing alone near the entrance. Twenty others also made full recoveries.

The girl returned to the men who'd sent her to the market. They unstrapped the bomb from around her stomach and dressed her in her own dress. She stayed with them for two weeks. Each night, they yanked the wounds from her body with sticks. She gained weight. The fear drained from her eyes. When she was fully healed, they brought her back to her village. They rebuilt her hut and the huts around it, and her family reappeared.

We have to go back to go forward, my therapist says. I take the little girl back further, until all she can see are colors and light.

I had three clients. The first was a red-haired, middle-aged tax processor with cirrhosis. His skin and eyes were yellow. He had a hard time remembering the simplest things. Mostly he wanted to watch me. I don't think he'd ever had a girlfriend. He said he'd had one who died. The second client was older, seventy probably. A talker, he kept trying to pick me up, as if....

It was five hundred dollars an hour. I had an ad on Craigslist. I made them take me to dinner first to make sure I was comfortable. I was eighteen; I hadn't even had sex until that year. My parents made such a big deal out of it for so long that when I finally did I was like it's my body, I'll do what I want with it.

I'd gotten kicked out of the dorms. It was so stupid. No more—or maybe just a little bit more—than what everybody else was doing. I saw myself as a person who was always getting caught, always getting blamed. I had to find a place, pay rent. I couldn't afford it. I thought I'd do anything to stay in New York. The funny thing is, I ended up having to go back home anyway.

It did leave scars. Nothing really bad ever happened. It could've been so much worse. I didn't get any diseases. No one strapped a bomb to my stomach. But I was angry for a long time. I wanted to go back. All the way, to before I was born, before my father and mother met, before the ships and the wars, all the way to Wallachia. A mountain village. A hut with a better version of myself inside. A myth.

The third client? I don't want to talk about him. I won't. It's private. Some things are still private, even after all these years. Even between you and me.

ENDNOTES

THE BROTHER

When I was small, say between the ages of four and ten, my sister, who's four years older, when she got annoyed with me she'd grab my wrists and with my own hands hit me in the head and face, all the while saying, "Why are you hitting yourself? Why are you hitting yourself?"

And I thought, I was sure, this would end when I got older, but here I am at age thirty-nine looking at pictures of my ex-wife, pictures of her at her mom's cabin on Lake Michigan, pictures of her in our old house, pictures of her running down a sand dune, pictures of her cross-legged on a motel bed, the comforter bunched around her waist, her pregnant stomach white in the over-bright motel light, and then, even though it's still light outside and I can hear my landlady talking to her mother on the phone downstairs, I lie down in bed on top of the comforter and curl my legs to my chest and think of the place on her shoulder where I used to rest my chin, the smell of her cheek, its softness, and behind the softness I hear my sister's voice.

THE SISTER

My brother holding his son's hand and his son trips and would've fallen but doesn't even realize because my brother catches him and swings him up with their joined arms so instead of falling his son is airborne for a moment swinging through the air.

All of this in a park near my home in Portland with an evening breeze rustling the sycamore leaves that hang low over the water.

Everyone here will die, they say—the young man on his back in the grass with his legs raised straight up to the sky, the young woman balanced on the soles of his feet, her arms outspread, the couple beyond them on a yellow blanket laughing until, red-faced, they look away.

Die as our parents died, as the little girl died, as the men who sent her to the market have, or will die. I watch the people in the park, my brother and his son. Blind men walking across a light-filled room.

WEEKI WACHEE, 1980

Lynnie and her boyfriend Sean pitched his tent, twisting the aluminum tubes together, female to male, and knocking stakes into sandy dirt with a mallet. Pine needles had sifted into its corners from the last time it was used. Since they were in charge of dinner the first night, they unpacked pasta and Ragu with Parmesan cheese in a green can. They'd brought two six-packs of Mexican beer and some limes. They'd stopped for boiled peanuts, sold out of the bed of a pickup truck en route to Weeki Wachee, the Florida state park that featured an underwater theater with live mermaid shows.

Lynnie's mother had brought her and her brother Jake to Weeki Wachee not long after their father died. That year they'd seen many of Florida's attractions, from Silver Springs to Cypress Gardens and Weeki Wachee. Mom was anti-Disney World. She didn't appreciate that the newer park had siphoned guests from every other attraction in Florida. They'd gone to see pelicans at Cedar Key and manatees wintering in Blue Spring State Park. They ate Key lime pie in Key West and passed a huge mound of conchs at a roadside stand. With age, Lynnie put it together that it must have been easier for her mom to tour Florida than to stay home. Lynnie's main memory of Key West was sitting on a round bench encircling a tree and Mom realizing their chicken was undercooked. It was bloody next to the bone.

Now the days had begun their slow shrink toward fall. This was Lynnie and Sean's last free summer before college graduation. Jake and his girlfriend Averie would cook the next night. Averie was applying to grad school after having worked for two years, and Jake was on vacation from his job that had something to do with computers. Since graduation, Averie had become more of a nature girl, more confident, talking at length about deltas and birds. Lynnie liked seeing them back together. She couldn't say when she'd first met Averie—one year their family had gone to the same inn as hers for Thanksgiving—but Jake and Averie had dated on and off through high school and college. With Jake's other girlfriends she didn't make conversation, not to be rude but because she had nothing to say. On the contrary, Averie had always put her at ease, asking her who she had for English, making a joke, or offering, "I like your t-shirt," and Lynnie would look down to see what shirt she was wearing since outfits weren't premeditated for her. Whenever Averie and Jake were broken up, he sounded philosophical: "Can't hate her—she's a part of my history." Lynnie felt Averie was part of her history, too. At some point, when she'd seen the carrot peel scab on Lynnie's shin, Averie had given her tips on how to shave her legs without bleeding. Averie had driven her to the mall to get her ears pierced. Lynnie missed having another girl around.

Sean set up the cooking equipment and put water on to boil. It wasn't easy for him to accept that for camping they'd make do with Ragu, but he looked to be consoling himself by doctoring it up with thyme and onion. He warmed garlic bread in foil packets tucked into the fire. He'd spent the summer before this one biking in France and learning to cook, and he still wore a fanny pack from time to time. He lived off campus, and that first evening he put his hand on the small of her back to guide her into the kitchen for paella, Lynnie felt the heat of his fingers under her thin shirt. While Sean cooked, the others scavenged for firewood, avoiding the palmettos because of snakes. The park was designed around the spring, laid out with campsites in one area and, in another, the underwater theater, built into the bank of the spring.

"I told my parents you and Averie would share a tent, and Jake and I would," Sean said over dinner.

"Why'd you need to explain it?" Lynnie asked. But then Sean looked deflated, and she smiled at him—no big deal, she promised. She hadn't meant to shame him.

"They asked about sleeping arrangements," he said.

"I wish I'd thought that up about the tents for my mother," Averie said. They all knew about her religious mother. Averie's thin, ash-blonde hair lay flat with humidity. She was prettier with a little age on her, and she had a lot of interests in her early twenties that she hadn't had before, for instance backpacking. She'd told them about the big weights she could carry on her back. She knew how to stay hydrated.

"Averie's mom didn't want her here without a ring on her finger," Jake said. He laughed, but he was too cavalier sometimes, and Lynnie thought that insensitive. Maybe Averie would like to be engaged a couple of years out of college. Jake didn't necessarily want to commit to one person, and when he talked about women, he always said he didn't need or want stock beauty. He had said he could be himself with Averie. But he didn't want to marry her, he'd told Lynnie earlier that summer. He didn't think their love measured up to Mom and Dad's. Lynnie understood him. She wouldn't want to get married now, either, not before having more experiences, more history. Mom and Dad had married young, but that had been a different generation. Back then premarital sex and cohabitation weren't allowed—even now they weren't officially allowed—and Mom and Dad had been too in love to wait.

Mom now showed hardly an interest in her children. She said food didn't taste good anymore. It was almost as if she'd decided to punish herself, to not enjoy any sensory pleasures if Dad was also unable to.

The moon bled blue tonight, floating in and out of shredded clouds.

"Pass the Parmesan," Jake said. Sean handed him the can.

"Best Ragu ever," Lynnie said, and Sean looked satisfied while the others hustled to agree. They'd finished off the beer and sucked the meat from all the boiled peanuts by the time Lynnie took out her camera because of the moon, the Sea of Tranquility a strong contrast tonight to the bright white lunar highlands. A cloud cupped the moon before trailing off in wisps.

"How's the photography?" Averie asked.

"I've got a new series." Lynnie told them about the box turtle she'd set under the blue plumbago in her mom's backyard, shot late afternoon when she could take advantage of shadows. She wished she'd brought her pictures so she could show Averie the turtle trapped in the pool, huddled inside its brown shell mapped with yellow starbursts, waiting for rescue. She'd lifted it out of the drain and onto the grass.

Soon even the combination of bug spray and campfire wasn't enough to keep the mosquitoes off them.

"I'm tired, anyway," Averie said.

"I'm full," Jake said.

They smothered the fire and locked the food in the chest because of raccoons. The couples said goodnight to each other. Sean spread a tarp on the tent floor, and they laid Lynnie's patchwork sleeping bag from childhood on top of his state-of-the-art L.L. Bean.

Lynnie knelt at the end of her bag and held the flashlight up to her chin. "Mwah, hah, hah," she said.

"Oooh, you scared me." Sean opened his eyes wide with "fear."

Lynnie turned on her camping lantern, heavy with its huge battery. Its light gave Sean's chest and arms a warm glow. They changed into boxers for Sean and an oversized t-shirt for Lynnie. She laid her head in the crook of his armpit. Sometimes she accidentally thought of him as a friend more than a lover. She felt his heart beating and didn't want to think about how vulnerable and excited he was.

"Mom brought us to Weeki Wachee once," she said. On that trip her mother had bought two mermaid plates "For Decorative Purposes Only." She had hung the plates above the stove until they grew sticky with dust, and when finally she hand washed them, the paint flaked off, the mermaids now only suggestions of themselves, "Weeki Wachee, Fla." nearly illegible.

"Was it fun?"

"My dad had just died of lung cancer, so no." Lynnie moved her head onto her pillow and turned on her side to face him.

"I didn't put that together," Sean said. He looked like he was searching out sadness on her face, and she tried to hide it from him as he traced the whorl of her ear with his finger. His hand smelled like garlic.

"Do you feel like you're just about to be a grownup?" she asked. "Like when you graduate, you'll suddenly be one?"

"No."

"Me, neither. I don't even like that word, 'grownup.' Or 'adult,' for that matter. It's like the word 'Mrs.' I would never want to be called 'Mrs.'"

"But don't you think you'll get married and have kids one day?" Sean asked.

"Why do you keep asking me that?"

"It's a normal question for two people together."

"Everything would be different if my dad were alive."

"Why's that? I mean, besides the obvious."

"It shows that planning ahead isn't very useful," Lynnie said.

"Are you saying we shouldn't look forward to stuff?"

"Never mind what I said. I'm buzzed. I would honestly get out my camera and shoot the moon some more, but my head's spinning." She flopped her arm over his bare chest and crooked her leg over his thighs. Her libido had gone into hiding.

"Tell me something else about you," he said.

She must have hesitated.

"Anything," he said.

Typical Sean—so nice, so interested. She reeled back in time to Jake and her as kids, just far enough apart in age that they didn't fight much, to her dad taking her to a turkey shoot, the shot that won her the camping lantern that lit the tent warm and orange now.

"There's my last clean-edged memory of him," she said.

Sean pulled back from her to be able to see her better when she described the Natural Springs Inn and its turkey shoot.

"Not a real turkey," she said. "A paper turkey, waiting to be shot across the spring. A man handed me a musket. I call it a musket, but maybe it wasn't. This gun—in my memory it was made out of the same wood as our piano. It made me think of the Civil War, though I can't tell you if it was a musket or a rifle or what. I was so grown up holding that gun. Grown up in the best way. I can still remember the weight of it in my hands, the delicate ring where I put my forefinger, and my dad telling me how to line up the two points. He was so excited when I shot the turkey."

"Thank you for telling me that," Sean said.

"A lot of my memories aren't in focus anymore. I remember the way he was—his mood, for example—more than specific things he said. I remember what he looked like, of course, but him in stills."

Now she saw him standing in his carport. He'd left behind a lot of lamps. A geode collection. None of the three kids had been attached to stuff like he had been. You can't take it with you, Mom would say, and she'd try to convince them that Dad's things weren't Dad, but as she proclaimed this, she got a funny uncomfortable look on her face as if she wasn't sure that was true. They all made efforts to clean out over the years, but mysteriously part of Dad did live through the lamps and the geodes. Besides that, he'd left architectural bits all over Jacksonville, mostly additions and renovations since they lived and he worked in an old part of town.

"I've almost forgotten his walk."

Billy Joel was right—only the good died young.

It was too hot to touch, so she rolled back from Sean and folded her sleeping bag away from her. Summer was too hot. She liked the spring and fall equinoxes when the world lost its tilt. But then she called up his slightly knock kneed walk, making his body seem even thinner. Some of his words floated around in her brain. A lot of the words he had left her were quotes from his favorite architects. *A house is a machine for living* (Le Corbusier). *Bring the outdoors in* (he had enrolled them in a Montessori school, and he claimed Maria Montessori said this, though Lynnie could never find a record of it). *I believe in God, only I spell it "Nature"* (Frank Lloyd Wright). *God is in the details* (Mies van der Rohe). She'd heard every one of these sayings multiple times by the time she turned 12. She wanted to live a quiet life in a cool house that was a machine for living, as her dad always made sure they knew Le Corbusier said a house should be.

"What?" Sean said.

"Nothing."

"You look deep in thought."

"Do you ever think about what kind of house you'd like to live in?" Lynnie asked.

"No, never," he said.

The frog ensemble swelled to a purr and mixed with the crickets scraping out a long-long-long pattern and then a short-short-short one. Sometimes the crickets and frogs sounded as if they were inside the tent.

"I'm tired," she said. "Night."

"I thought we'd—"

"I'm tired. I'm buzzed. My brother's in the next tent over."

"I understand," Sean said.

The next morning the sun woke her up, her shoulder wet with condensation against the nylon wall. She unzipped their tent to find Averie by the dead fire.

"Go with me?" Averie was holding a clear plastic toiletries bag and swung her arm toward the bathhouse.

"Sure." Lynnie ducked back into the tent for her stuff. They walked along the path, both still half-asleep, not talkative yet. Oxidized spots mottled the wall-sized mirror, while paint hung from the walls as if skin peeling after sunburn. Lynnie picked a hair from her Old Spice stick.

"Sean's," she said. "He forgot his toothbrush and used mine. God, we sound like an old married couple."

Averie said she liked Secret brand deodorant. They leaned toward the mirror and brushed their teeth with sink water so freezing that Lynnie's teeth hurt. She was taller than Averie. Today she was wearing flip-flops, but she regularly wore ballet slippers as shoes—she owned pairs in pink, black, and tan to be more on the girl height bell curve.

"You think this is spring-fed?" Lynnie asked.

"Cold enough to be," Averie said.

Once done with her brief routine, Lynnie sat on the bar of sinks, her back to the mirror. She watched Averie curl her hair. She wasn't jealous of Averie. She didn't look at beautiful women or bodies competitively, like fashion magazines implied and sociologists claimed women did. She never saw a woman as a threat, judging her clothes, hair, or looks. Women weren't threats but were lovely. No surprise there were so many mermaids and few mermen. Averie sprayed either side of her wide forehead. The hairspray smell made Lynnie think of the church retreat at the Sea Turtle Inn, where she'd lost her virginity, her hips pointy against his. His youth group was visiting from somewhere in the Panhandle. The bamboo nightstand table next to her had a dusty glass top. She remembered both twins—the other one a sister, unnaturally tan with teased hair that had an artificial green apple smell. She wrote them, and they didn't write her back.

Lynnie leaned back against the mirror. "I've never used one of those," she said about the curling iron.

"I could teach you."

"Sure." She skidded off the counter and faced the mirror again.

"I wouldn't bother," Averie said, "except for my hair's so flat and thin." Shorter than Lynnie, Averie stood behind her shoulder and parceled out a piece of hair. She trapped it in the curling iron, slid the iron to the end of the piece of hair, and rolled it up. "Tell me if I'm burning your head," she said.

"I've got a high pain threshold."

"Good thing." Averie unrolled the iron, leaving one side of Lynnie's hair a tube wave. "Now you try it." Averie held her hand over Lynnie's to demonstrate how the clamp worked.

When Lynnie's thumb tired, she set the iron on the counter and patted her new hair. "Good enough." She pointed toward her head. "Is this an improvement?"

"You're a natural kind of girl, more than a priss."

"I don't know if this is me, but thank you." Then Lynnie gave Averie a loose hug, as Southern girl-women do to thank each other or to say hello or goodbye, close enough for Lynnie to smell Averie's toothpaste and to feel a pull toward her that was more than a swelling of appreciation for help with hair, and then, without thinking it through, Lynnie held Averie's upper arms, muscly from backpacking—she smelled good—mint toothpaste plus some fresh citrus—and Lynnie bent her knees, closed her eyes, and kissed Averie on the mouth.

Averie did not return the kiss—instead she stiffened and pulled back with a confused look. She wiped her mouth with the back of her hand, let out an awkward burst of a laugh, and then looked to be repressing any further reaction. They both faced the mirror. Lynnie kept her eyes on her own new hair, dark and bloated against her skin, which was burned to tan, as she ranged around for words to explain away what had happened. She couldn't find any. Sean was one of those people who kissed acquaintances hello on the lips—maybe she could explain it away that way. She had wanted to be pretty for Averie as much as she had for Sean.

"Sorry about that." Lynnie packed up her toiletries.

"It's okay," Averie said.

"I don't know what that was."

"It was weird," Averie said.

"I know."

They walked more than arms' length from each other back toward the campsite. She had no idea where the urge to kiss Averie had come from. It scared her. They were too quiet, and she blurted,

"How about that moon last night?"

Averie started to say something. "Never mind," she said. Her look was guarded, unfamiliar.

Why had Lynnie brought up the moon, the female controller of tides? She hadn't set out to make suggestive or romantic conversation with Averie.

In their absence the guys had started breakfast: little smokies and eggs. Lynnie felt Sean's eyes following her.

"You look great," he said finally. "Wow."

"It's temporary," Lynnie said.

"But still."

Her eyes watered when Sean grabbed her hand.

After breakfast they followed the path toward the underwater theater, ordered their tickets, and bought gum shaped like oranges in the gift shop. They found seats. Right away Sean put his arm around Lynnie, and Averie nudged Jake to put his around her, like she was in some couples' competition or, worse, protecting herself from Lynnie. It wasn't as if they lived in California or New York City. They weren't from Miami or Key West but were thirty miles from the Georgia border. It would be 35 years before same-sex marriage would be legalized in Florida, years before AIDS and Don't Ask Don't Tell would wax and wane in the news, and decades before gay couples would hold hands at Jacksonville Beach and not be quarantined in the windowless AJ's and Coral Reef bar. In 1980 Jacksonville, Catholics were religious diversity and all the Jewish people lived on the South Side. There were only five Black students in her high school and no Black members in the golf and country clubs. Secret clusters of little old ladies nominated debutantes, and tattoos on the middle to upper class did not exist. In another 20 years, several of her high school classmates would come out as gay. But in 1980, no one had come out in her high school. Nor in her small Southern liberal arts college. She'd had a little internal question about the occasional gym teacher or church worker with men's haircuts, sports jerseys, never married, living alone or with a roommate. But she was nothing like them. She knew that things were very different in places like San Francisco, but here androgyny was under suspicion.

Soon the first mermaids swam into view behind the thick glass, using hoses to breathe. Disappointingly, they didn't have tails but were swimmers Lynnie's mother's age with legs and feet. They advertised Florida orange juice, pretending to drink it. In one of Lynnie's science fair projects, she'd found the Vitamin C levels practically nil in store-bought juice compared to fresh-squeezed, and Lynnie had a fleeting appreciation for her mother's having always squeezed their juice fresh. The mermaids made her think of her mother swimming freestyle in her cotton suit, made before Lycra or rayon, or whatever the quick-drying fabrics were, her car seat invariably wet after the drive home from the beach.

Now young mermaids swam out wearing tails—finally!— the sun casting a fishnet latticework on their shoulders and breasts. Some combination of ballerina, gymnast, and swimmer, they lifted each other into patterns of bodies both geometric and organic. Lynnie thought of her mother's mouth in a kumquat-sized "O," her tanned arms with their hint of alleged Seminole, hinging easily at the elbow. Since Daddy died, her mother had hardly swum at all. Every mermaid pointed her toes.

The mermaids' hair flowed, suspended in the water, Earth's master hairstylist. Lynnie sneaked a look at Averie, whose curls had relaxed in the humidity. She was worrying about what Averie thought of her, fretting she'd lose this friend and afraid Averie would tell the guys. She didn't think of Averie as a gossip, but she wondered if she ought to ask her not to say anything back home. She eased her camera and telephoto lens out of their big bag, opened a new box of film, and spread its tail over the sprockets. She closed the back of the camera and bent over it to muffle the loud crunch the advance lever would make in the amphitheater as she forwarded the film to one. If only she could reverse advance the day, unfurl its film from its sprockets like some time machine back to before the moment in the bathhouse with Averie.

It was easier having her camera in front of her face than it was to keep her expression natural for the others. One mermaid lifted another, her hand on the small of the other's back, which was so arched that her rib cage looked like wings. Bubbles rose from both of their lips. Someone should design a quieter shutter. Her father would have appreciated that thought. Two more mermaids sat at the mouth of a great shell and made looks of horror when a male sea dragon appeared.

Jake was whispering to Averie now and not watching the show. Averie took Jake's hand, the one that was over her shoulder, and pulled it further in around her. Meanwhile, over a crackling loudspeaker, a voice educated them about the Weeki Wachee River: the cypress, the egrets, the family of peacocks, the Underwater Grand Canyon, and the mermaids fighting the current in this, the deepest spring in the United States. The scratchy voice informed them that Weeki Wachee translated to "little spring" or "winding river" in Seminole, and that the swimmer in the opening scene of *Jaws* had been a Weeki Wachee mermaid.

Late afternoon, the guys wanted to check out the newly opened Buccaneer Bay, and they all four went to the white-sand beach. Lynnie wore her ancient swim team suit, a green and white Speedo with a pattern that made her think of pieced-together family crests, each about one-and-a-half inches wide. She'd always gotten a gradual tan under the white parts of a Speedo. One year her suit had been striped, and she'd tanned in stripes. She hitched up her suit on her thigh to show Averie this summer's tan crests. When Averie laughed awkwardly, she regretted having done so.

Averie wore a striped bikini with wooden rings at the hips and between her breasts. She squeezed a pool of baby oil into her cupped hand and used two fingers to spread it around and under the edges of her bikini. Tans were important in this state, but Lynnie didn't care enough to mess with baby oil to attract the sun. Averie already had a good base, what with her rare tan skin/ blond combination like a Scandinavian. She struggled to reach the middle of her back.

Lynnie knew not to help Averie with her back. She lay on her towel and closed her eyes, everything red behind them. She had lost all ability to make conversation or to interact naturally with Averie. She heard Averie turning pages of a magazine. After a while, she propped herself up on her elbows to look for the guys, who'd been riding down the water slide. She should have done that with them instead of laying out. She recognized both their walks as they approached—Jake flat-footed and slouched—maybe he was trying to take up less space in the world, same as she was. Stocky Sean walked erectly to gain height. She made it a point not to look at Averie. The slide would have been more fun than this. Jake stopped and shook his dark head like a dog, the way he always did after he'd been in water.

"I'm afraid Jake and I are headed for a break-up again," Averie said.

"Why do you say that?"

Now Lynnie looked. Averie shook her head, her eyes light and dark brown like bird's eye maple. Lynnie was relieved she was speaking to her, and yet she wondered what Averie was doing. Was she testing her, saying aloud whatever random thought floated across her consciousness to see what kind of reaction she could get? Averie would know Lynnie was loyal to Jake—but then she was loyal to Averie, as well.

When the guys were back, "We ought to get dinner started," Averie said to Jake. The tops of his shoulders were already burning. He agreed about dinner, and their two figures receded down the wooden boardwalk that led to the campsite. Lynnie sat up on her knees.

"I was watching you earlier." Sean flopped down beside her. "I'd like to see that tan line." He reached for her thigh.

"Don't." Lynnie held down the leg holes of her suit. She didn't want him to touch her. She didn't deserve him, anyway, not when she had half-longed for a girl who belonged to her brother, not when she was tanned with these crests like scales.

"You're sweaty." She dabbed at a rivulet that drained from his temple.

"I've got something to ask you," he said.

Her knees ached. She hoped this didn't mean he knew about Averie. Maybe he was going to ask something innocuous like what she really thought about last night's dinner or how often she thought they'd be able to see each other the last week of summer. And yet the way he had said *something to ask you* had given her body a dropping sensation, like chills after sunburn. She'd be good now, she'd do as he asked—she would be the good girlfriend and sister and friend and pretend she was free of unconventional urges. She regretted snapping at him about the tan line.

Sean dropped to his knees, to be her same height, she assumed. He unzipped the cargo pocket of his swim shorts and held out a small round object, which she soon saw was an alligator twisted into a ring, its snout kissing the tip of its tail. That was cute. That was funny. Sweet of Sean to think of her at the gift shop, though he shouldn't have wasted his money. But no matter how much of an amusing oddity the ring, Sean looked serious as he said, "Will you marry me, Lynnie Byrd?"

Lynnie had a surreal focus on his lips and teeth as he formed those six words. This was unexpected. This wasn't right. She forced a smile. "I'm very flattered," she said.

"Lately I've felt you slipping away," he said.

"I haven't supported myself yet. I've never lived alone."

"I'd like to know that we're together, that you're part of my future."

"Pretty unusual to get engaged before graduation." She

stood up and shook the sand from her towel. Sean's jaw clenched, and she kept her eyes on it, almost compelled to see the hurt she'd caused.

"Is that a 'no?'" he asked.

"Just a 'not yet,'" she said.

Then he looked so disappointed that she turned her back on him and ran. When she heard his solid footsteps behind her, she about-faced and took him by the forearms. "Please don't follow me. I need a minute alone."

Now his eyes looked unfocused on the distance.

"It's not you—it's me," she said. There was a reason some breakup lines became clichés—because they were true.

She took off again, running barefoot on the sandy soil littered with pine needles and yelling in pain when she trod on a pinecone. But she kept leaping for pinecones as if they were stones across a river. She welcomed the distraction and deserved the pain. She passed palmettos and the stadium, crashed through some weeds, and dove into the mermaid pool, which was so cold that the breath nearly knocked out of her. She had no investment in her beautiful stroke but jerked through the water as fast as she could, trying to warm up but unable to. She was like one of those long-limbed insects skimming the spring. She couldn't hear her heartbeat or her breath for the water that rushed from the spring at gallons per second.

Was she shortsighted? Sean was a good person in love with her. He was *nice*, a word she hated whenever it was applied to her. He would be a smart long-term choice, a man for the future. He could save her.

She tried to swim all in one plane like a mermaid, legs sealed together in butterfly kick toward the cave. The crystal clear water was nothing like the warmer Atlantic—no Sea of Tranquility, this cold water. She never warmed up to comfortable, and as she scrambled out of the water, trying to catch her breath, she realized the mermaids must have been freezing. They must have trained themselves to smile like that.

The sun was setting, sky pink, and dinner nearly ready by the time she made it back to the campsite. Maybe Sean had asked Jake to explain her.

What is it with your sister? Sean might have lobbed at Jake.

She couldn't explain herself, and her brother wouldn't do any better. For a second she thought from Averie's expression and a searching look from Jake that Sean had told them he'd been rejected. Maybe Averie had even detailed the moment in the bathroom, revealed Lynnie's mention of the moon. But no, dinner unfolded without any reference to the proposal or the bathhouse. Jake brought up *The Incredible Hulk* pilot where the Hulk comes across a father and daughter camping, and that segued into several unoriginal ghost stories. Soon they were debating whether or not marshmallows were food. Sean, energized by this argument, said they absolutely were not food as he thrust one into the fire. Everyone was acting normally, eating marshmallows raw and cooked. Lynnie finally realized Sean wouldn't have told Jake because of pride. With a throe of sadness for him, she knew that he was still pursuing her, that she was slipping away, and that he had no idea what her problem was. She moved over to his log and twisted toward him. He stared at either his marshmallow or the fire as if it were most fascinating. She watched his marshmallow catch on fire. He brought it toward him and blew out the flame. Averie said she couldn't take the mosquitoes anymore, and she and Jake kicked off their shoes outside their tent and went inside it.

"You okay?" Lynnie skated her hand over Sean's thigh. She closed her eyes and focused on her lips on his, making the kiss as sweet and loving as she could, as passionate as possible, but it was intellectual—she was overthinking it, her tongue in search of something she could call truth.

"Where'd that come from?" he asked. She shrugged. He slid the blackened skin from his marshmallow and ate it, then offered her the middle. She said yes, please!

"I'm glad they don't know about this," he said.

"Me, too. I'm sorry."

It wasn't his fault that she was abnormal—and she was so sorry for him.

When his chin dimpled with emotion, she pulled him toward their tent. She pressed her body to his. He was backlit by the camping lantern, his face in shadow. The world was tilted as much as it ever had been, the light behind her closed eyelids more burnt orange than warm glow. The sex wasn't bad for guilt sex, and with the effort to keep the others from hearing. She hoped through that thick glass she'd gotten the mermaids on film.

ORPHAN MARKDOWN

They liked to chill at the skate park in their hoodies and low-slung jeans, doing ollies and rail-slides, smoking cigarettes, blowing on their hands to warm them. When it got too cold, they'd head over to Comic Haven to antagonize the thick-lensed halitosic nerds until the owner eighty-sixed them. Then they'd jet to Perkins for the bottomless pot of coffee and maybe a plate of eggs and hash browns between them if they could scrounge enough change. They dropped acid once in a while but nobody had anything right now, not even any decent pot. Their supplier, Sir Dancelot, was vacationing in Vail with his bail bondsman. Nobody had any beer, and the effort to track down someone with a valid ID willing to buy them beer without tacking on a grotesquely unjust surtax was more than they could stomach. Tonight pretty much every citizen in town was watching the high school football game, participating in it, copping feels under the bleachers, or messing with the opposing team's cars in the parking lot. None of those options appealed to the crew.

"Maybe we could hotwire some golf carts at the country club and drive them into the pond."

"We could huff some paint thinner."

"Or watch that porno again, the one with the double-jointed midget."

The crew nuked some pizza rolls and mulled things over.

"Maybe we could check out one of the orphanages." This from Trip, the most diminutive member of the group. His parents had long ago divorced, and his mom was now an over-aerobicized walking infomercial, the owner of a 24 hour fitness club in the strip mall out by the bypass, in a former video store with sneaker-scuffed tiles and scored marks on the wall notating where shelving units once stood—new releases, thrillers, horror, comedies, all of life's major genres. Old video cases were still stacked in a corner of the break room, the final carapaces of a race of creatures driven to extinction by the digital era. Trip's mom was always either working the front desk or the Nautilus machines or competing in regional aerobi-thons, so Trip was virtually an orphan himself.

"What would we do at an orphanage?" Taylor said.

"Look at the kids, I guess."

"Jesus, Trip, they're not like puppies at the mall," Seth said.

"The pet shop at the mall closed down," someone pointed out.

Trip's eyes shone in an aqueous way. "I know they're not puppies. I just want to see them, that's all. They probably don't get many visitors."

"Which one would we go to? Aren't there like seven out on County Line?"

"Don't forget the ones by the courthouse."

"I say we head to County Line," Brock said. "Better neighborhood." Brock was their unacknowledged leader. Everyone knew that once he cut his hair and started doing homework, his ascent would be swift.

The town was quiet. A lone shopping cart with an ad circular clinging to its leg drifted aimlessly through the supermarket parking lot, some kids lit a string of firecrackers in the dead grass outside the fixed-rent apartment complex, a couple waitresses passed listlessly back and forth behind the blazing panes of glass at the Perkins like the world's saddest figure skaters. Buildings gradually slid away until only a few scattered lights remained. The football stadium, floodlights blazing, sat atop a distant hill like a citadel, something held aloft for praise. The other hills looked like shadowy cutouts under a purplish sky, a moon the color of crab-meat hanging at the edges.

The first of the orphanages appeared. The sign out front said simply KIDS, bracketed in neon, a string of Christmas lights stapled along the roofline. It was the cinder-blocked, deep win-dowed den of a psychic or palm reader, someone who preyed on those with little to give. As usual, Brock articulated what the others were thinking. "Let's find something a little more tasteful."

What the next orphanage lacked in sophistication, it made up for in size, housed in a prefab structure of monolithic propor-tions with a massive parking lot including gas pumps at the far end and a convenience kiosk as though visitors might need to refuel be-fore reaching the front entrance. It looked like a supercenter where people bought toilet paper in bulk. Several busses were parked near the front doors and kids exited the orphanage single-file in match-ing blaze orange pajamas, backpacks slung over their shoulders, boarding the Trailways. "Nope," Brock said. "Keep going."

The third place appeared well-tended but unassuming. Seth, piloting his mom's minivan, turned in and parked next to the lone bus in the lot. "You think there'll be nuns?" he asked, but no one knew the answer to that.

There were no nuns. Instead, a rangy fellow who resembled an extra in a John Ford Western stood on a stepstool watering a hanging plant, exhaling the fumes of an unfiltered cigarette into the foliage. Without turning, he said, "Here for a pickup?"

"We want to check out the orphans," Trip said, looking to his friends for confirmation. They were busy picking at old skateboarding scabs or studying the water-stained ceiling panels. For some reason Trip had put the hood of his sweatshirt up, cinching it tight so it framed his face, the fleshy lips and long feminine lashes, as though he were gazing through a porthole.

The night manager climbed down from his stool and gave everyone the once-over. It was so quiet they could hear the hum of the outdated computer behind the counter. "Check them out?" The man smiled as he ambled across the room to stow the stepstool in a closet. "This ain't a lending library."

"Yes, Sir—" Trip began, but the night manager cut him off.

"I know what you meant, son." He addressed the group. "Why aren't you at the ballgame?"

"We're not into football," Brock said.

"Me neither. Just a lot of meaningless squabbling if you ask me. So you want to see the kids, huh? What for?"

"We just thought it'd be nice to talk to them for a minute," Taylor said. "You know, about school and stuff."

The night manager seemed skeptical. "Are you getting extra credit or something?" The boys shrugged or looked away, not wanting to lie. "I guess there's no harm in it," he said finally, "but you'll have to wait until the gentleman from United Bauxite is done. Mr. Forsythe's closing a package deal."

The crew slid into some contoured vinyl chairs that looked like they'd been snatched up at a Laundromat liquidation sale, ashtrays built into the armrests. "These would be cool for parties," Seth commented. It felt weird seeing people smoking in such numbers again, but with the civil suits squelched and the sin taxes repealed, cigarettes were cheap commodities. Last year's Super Bowl-winning quarterback could be seen in a TV ad, casually holding a smoldering cigarette as he walked a tropical beach with his supermodel girlfriend. The cigarette companies no longer had to include those pesky warnings about the dangers of nicotine, low birth weights, all that hoopla, and the industry was booming. Camels and Kools could be bought in vending machines by pretty much anyone with a couple bucks to spare.

Taylor had an uncle Louis who spouted conspiracy theories every holiday. One of his favorites was that cigarettes were a voter suppression tool, their "pushers" operating at the highest levels. "Look who's dying from them," he said. "Poor folks, minorities, artistic types. All the thorns in the administration's side, killing themselves a pack at a time. Hell, those bastards in Washington would probably mix antifreeze with asbestos and peddle it in pill form if they thought they could get away with it." Uncle Louis would of course be haloed in smoke as he said this, pausing to let loose a rattling nicotine-laden cough.

The man from United Bauxite emerged with the orphanage owner, Forsythe, whom they recognized from his gilt-framed picture hanging over the cash drawer and his car dealer-style ads on local TV. "Bring us your tired, your weak, your orphan masses," he would say, costumed as Uncle Sam, pointing a bony finger at the camera. Forsythe made it sound as though a woman's civic duty was to give up her unplanned child. He was very convincing. Even now the owner smooth-talked and glad-handed the United Bauxite man, trying to close the deal when it appeared the deal was already closed. Trailing behind was a gaggle of little foundlings in PJs and comfy slippers, prepared for the all-night ride to the United Bauxite compound, all of them dragging along their kid-sized luggage. Boys, mainly, a few girls tossed in for good measure. It was rumored the orphanages liked to close these big deals on nights and weekends, when the flow of children out the door wasn't quite so conspicuous. The owners also liked to catch kids when they were drowsy, like farmers rounding up roosting hens for the butcher. The United Bauxite man called to his assistant, a fine-boned woman in a gauzy dress that looked like it might come unraveled with a single strong tug. She was the type one saw at private galleries or wine tastings. "I've got to settle up accounts with Mr. Forsythe here," said the UB man. "Why don't you get the kids loaded onto the bus?"

There was an exchange of paperwork at the front counter, an invoice with yellow and pink duplicates. As Forsythe soldiered on with the forms, the United Bauxite man took a look at the crew seated opposite him.

"We're not for sale," Brock said mildly.

The man flashed them a smile. "Too bad. I bet you'd take to our refineries like ducks to water."

Mr. Forsythe glanced up. "Harry, what are these youngsters doing here?"

"They're here to look at the kids," said the night manager, leaning on the counter.

Mr. Forsythe's face told everyone he was striving to keep things pleasant. "This isn't a nature preserve. Hair is combed, teeth are brushed, kids are in bed excepting those our friend here has chosen for his company's needs. They've just won themselves a life as productive citizens." A nod to the United Bauxite man, who was viewing things with a certain degree of mirth.

"Forsythe," he said, "you may as well take them through. It will be a formative experience. See how the other half lives, so to speak."

And so it was settled, Forsythe doing what was required to grease the wheels of commerce. "Yes," he replied, "you're probably right. Harry, go ahead and give them a tour, but quietly and quickly, please."

Harry entered some numbers on a keypad by the door and beckoned the crew to follow. The inner chamber smelled of tightly embroiled childhood, a mix of talcum powder and no-tears shampoo; beneath that the slow mold of wet towels and sweat socks; and, another stratum below, the various secretions and discharges, toe jam and urine, a layer cake of aromas.

Bunks were spaced closely together, barracks-style, with what appeared to be a nurse's station in the corner, and the younger children, those not chosen in the United Bauxite draft, tossed and turned, attempting to identify their final sleep positions. The overhead lights had been dimmed but a few small lamps burned as the older kids lay reading tattered paperbacks. The empty, just-vacated beds spaced randomly around the room were jarring, like a stranger who suddenly smiles to reveal a mouthful of missing teeth. This must've been the boys' quarters, for there were no girls in evidence. Lying on their sides, some of the kids regarded the tourists passing through with the expressionless gazes of zoo apes.

"Can we talk to them?" Seth asked.

"Sure," said Harry. "Just keep your voices low and don't disturb the sleeping ones."

But none of them could think of much to say, so they merely nodded to the children, who returned their greetings with leaden solemnity, muttering hellos.

"How much does one cost?" Trip asked within earshot of the kids.

"It all depends," Harry answered, ignoring the indelicacies of the question. "Individual adoption rates hold pretty steady. Always about the same number of couples can't have kids of their own. The rate's actually gone down a bit since Washington stopped letting same sex couples adopt. Money these days is in the corporate sector. Ever since the deportations started on the immigrant front, there's been a big uptick in demand. Harvesting, fruit-picking, working the canneries, you name it. Washington dropped the minimum wage; that helped. So did letting some slack into the child labor laws."

"So how much does one cost?" Brock said, uninterested in the economics. They were standing at the far end of the barracks, near a communal white-tiled bathroom and shower where a few stragglers were still scrubbing behind their ears or spitting toothpaste into the gleaming basins. A shaft of fluorescent light stretched from the doorway, reaching partway across a boy's Star Wars coverlet. The child sat up in bed, watching them with round raccoon-y eyes, hands clasped over his stomach. His face appeared flushed, and a green dewdrop of snot dangled from one nostril.

"Healthy ones with normal IQs and a documented provenance can fetch upward of five to ten grand," Harry said, regarding the boy with the runny nose. "It ranges downward from there."

"What's the cheapest one you've got?" Trip asked.

"Well, this one here—" Harry motioned toward the child who sat watching them—"someone could probably snag him for as little as eight-hundred or a thousand bucks."

"Wow," Seth said. "That's a pretty good bargain for a living person."

"No doubt," Harry agreed. "The organs alone are worth more than that. Of course," he added, lowering his voice, "we don't condone harvesting. These are all good kids who deserve loving homes." Harry began guiding them back toward the door. "Orphanages were nearly phased out there for a while. The trend was in foster care, people taking kids in just to snag a little public assistance. But now the laws have changed and the foster care system can't keep up. Too many unwanteds. That's where the private sector steps in to save the day. We provide a valuable service, generate some tax revenues, the spirit of competition keeps rates down."

Trip kept looking over his shoulder at the runny-nosed boy still visible in the light cast by the bathroom. "You're telling me I could get that kid back there for eight-hundred bucks? You can't even get a Peavey half-stack for eight-hundred."

Harry laughed. "I'm saying someone probably could. A grown-up. Of legal age."

"There's a law against teens adopting?" Brock asked.

Harry massaged his chin stubble. "This is hypothetical, right? I mean, there was a law, but there've been some new statutes lately, so I'm not positive. I'm not really the one to talk to. You'd have to check with a lawyer. But this is all hypothetical, right?"

"You already asked that," Taylor said.

*

"Dude," Seth exclaimed as they crossed the parking lot, gravel crunching underfoot. "We could totally buy that kid." They climbed into his mom's minivan.

"What would we do with him?" Brock asked.

"Teach him how to skate," Trip said. "Show him some guitar riffs. Sign him up for the Webelos. You know, normal kid stuff."

"Plus I bet you could teach him to pick up your room," Seth added. "Do your laundry, take out the garbage, a few chores to earn his keep."

"You guys are whacked," Taylor said. "Kids need a mom and dad."

"All I've got is my mom," Trip argued, "and she's never around."

"Me too," Seth admitted.

"There are four of us," Brock said. "That's like twice as good as a mom and dad. Besides, look who's taking care of these kids now: a couple old dudes who are just going to sell them to a corporation that wants them for picking lettuce or whatever."

"It takes a village," Seth said.

"What?" Taylor said. "What does that mean? How are we going to come up with eight-hundred bucks? This is insane. What good is a kid to us? What do we get out of it? It just sounds like a lot of work."

"Companionship," Brock said. "He'd be our little bro'."

"Companionship!" Taylor repeated. He had brought the

volume level up a notch. He had become animated. "Get a dog. We can keep it at my house. I'll even take it for walks." There was a click as his seatbelt came unlatched.

"Keep your seatbelt on," Seth called from the driver's seat.

"We'll make a trade," Brock said. "Taylor's parents' big-screen for the kid."

"What?!" Taylor convulsed in his seat, but at least he'd re-buckled. "Don't you think they'd notice their TV is missing? And who says that Forsythe guy would trade anyhow?"

"Think about it," Brock said. "The longer Forsythe keeps those kids around, the longer he's got to feed them, clothe them, pay their dental bills. He benefits from a quick turnover. Haven't you ever watched the house flipping shows? It's like that, but with kids. And this one's obviously not going anywhere. It's a win-win. Forsythe gets a new flat-screen for the orphanage, plus he offloads a hard-to-offload kid."

"Ever wonder why the kid's so cheap?" Taylor asked the others. "Maybe there's something wrong with him. Did you notice how he didn't say anything? Maybe he's retarded. Or remember that movie about the orphan kid who killed her parents? Maybe he's psychotic. Besides, you never said how we're going to make the TV disappear without my parents freaking."

"That's easy," Brock said. "We'll stage a break-in."

The streets were filled with people leaning out of car windows, yelling and honking, laying rubber, hurling obscenities at the kid working the Taco Bell drive-thru, which could only mean the town's football squad had won. Inside Taylor's house, the teens donned some rubber gloves they found under the sink and were now moving through the rooms, scattering CDs, overturning furniture, opening cupboards and drawers.

As they strained under the weight of the big-screen, maneuvering it awkwardly down the steps and across the lawn, they saw a couple classmates heaving rolls of TP into a sycamore two houses down—Don Cramer, who helped them with their algebra homework; and Tony Mostolli, better known as "Butterball." The crew wedged the TV into the rear of the minivan and nodded to the vandals, who silently pumped their fists in the air. Solidarity. Then Butterball winged another roll.

A number of pre-Halloween pumpkins had been sacrificed to the gods of victory, their orangey rinds scattered over the road. Occasionally the pale countenances of revelers and mischief-makers appeared in the van's headlights like some bacchanalian dream, but Seth kept the pedal down as they drove back to the orphanage. Already the would-be parents had matured to the point where such juvenile antics were beneath them.

They panicked, however, when they saw the new bus in the parking lot, a gleaming silvery vehicle with a Coors logo on its flank. "We've got to get in there," Trip said. Seth and Brock were already unloading the big-screen. They could picture the Coors man plucking their orphan out from under them to work the assembly line in some bottling plant or harvest wheat in the North Dakota tundra. Their runny-nosed bro' would not fare well in the northern plains.

"Whoa, there," Harry said, holding up a cautionary hand when he saw the crew and its cargo. Seth was sweating and swaying under the weight of the TV, which gradually came to rest on the floor of the lobby like a ship coming to ground. It really was a monstrous thing with a movie theater-sized screen. "What are you bringing that in here for? Are you going to be a problem?"

"Just the opposite," Brock said, emerging from behind the TV. "We're here to offer you a solution, a bargain. An exchange, if you will. The boy in back with the runny nose and the Star Wars comforter for this almost-new Samsung big-screen hi-def TV." Brock was really laying their cards on the table. Maybe that was how business was done; none of the others were entirely sure.

Harry came around the counter and circled the TV as though it were a prize heifer at a livestock auction, lifting its tail, eyeing its haunches appraisingly. "Does it work?" he asked.

Trip scrambled for an outlet. There ensued a tense moment where the crew feared the remote had been forgotten before Taylor reluctantly withdrew it from his jacket pocket. Harry produced an antenna, and soon they were entranced before CSI: Detroit in all its lustrous hues.

"What in the good Christ?" Forsythe said, startling them, though there was not any rancor in his voice.

"The boys here brought it in," Harry said, pointing a thumb toward the screen. "Good picture, wouldn't you say?"

"They just brought it in, huh? Doing their part for charitable causes?"

Harry smiled, and his mustache did a little dance. "They've got a proposition for you."

"This ought to be good," Forsythe said, glancing back toward the door to the orphanage's inner sanctum, where presumably the Coors man was traveling bunk to bunk, noting pulses and head circumferences and breathing sounds with the company doctor. The procedure for picking children when they all lay with blankets up to their throats seemed mysterious, capricious, but then every child was a little bit of a crapshoot, being unformed clay and all that.

"We're willing to swap you the TV for your most inexpensive child, the dark-eyed boy in the corner," Brock said. "Think what this big-screen would do for your orphanage's common room. The kids would love it."

"This isn't a pawn shop," Forsythe said. "We don't take trade." He turned back toward the dormitory.

"You can't?" Seth said, "Or you just don't want to? Because is there any rule that states a trade can't be negotiated? This is a fifteen-hundred dollar TV we're talking about, and we know for a fact the child's only worth eight-hundred or so."

Forsythe glanced at Harry, who looked away. "What do you want with the kid? His name's Oriel, by the way. You're not into sick stuff, are you? I could call the cops right now and find out. I'm on a bowling team with Detective Fellowes. I could ask him to pull your files."

"We don't have files," Brock assured him, "and we're not into sick stuff. We just think we could do a good job of raising little Oriel. And you get a state of the art TV in return. It's a win-win."

"It's not hot, is it?" Forsythe asked.

Trip went over and felt the set. "No, room temperature."

Forsythe let go a frustrated exhalation of breath. "No, I meant…" The sentence petered out. They all watched the show for a moment. Some porn music was playing while a sexy CSI analyzed evidence under a microscope. "Harry, what do you think? Is this by the book?"

Harry shrugged, but it was easy to see he'd already become wedded to the set. His eyes kept returning to it. The icy cold reaches of urban Detroit, by way of the Samsung folks, was just too alluring to ignore. "We could give the counselor a call, I suppose," he offered half-heartedly.

"I don't know," Forsythe said. He was like the lab rat that knew it'd be shocked if it reached for the cheese, but oh how he wanted that cheese. "Boys, let me think on it some. I've got to go in and seal this deal, but once that's done we'll talk."

In the end—after a true crime program and the evening news, after the Coors man led away his single-file flock to the silver bullet bus out front, after the crew was made to sign paperwork assuming its collective responsibility for Oriel's care, forms acknowledging the lawful exchange of goods, an impromptu affidavit attesting that the TV was not in fact stolen—the adoption came to pass, all within the span of about an hour and a half. "I can't believe it was that easy," Brock said. "I waited longer to get my driver's license."

Trip wrapped an arm around the boy's shoulders as they walked together toward the minivan. Oriel had been awakened from a fitful, wheezing slumber and was still in his pajamas, which were of the tight matching two-piece variety, with scores of little faded Buzz Lightyears on them. He was too old for such sleepwear. He rubbed the sleep from his eyes, snozzled the snot when it threatened to drip from his nose. His slippers scuffed against the pavement as he walked. His possessions, such as they were, filled a single duffle bag, which Seth tossed in back.

"This is awesome!" Seth said. "Our very own kid. We can let him do all the cool shit our parents never let us do. We can let him watch all the Friday the 13th movies."

"Hey Fartface," Brock said, "watch your language. We don't want him picking up all your potty talk."

"Where should we go?" Seth asked. "I feel like we should find a party or something. Trial by fire, right?"

"You can't take a kid to a party," Taylor grumbled.

"Why not?" Seth said.

"Look at him." They all turned to observe Oriel, curled now in a fetal position in the way-back, covering himself with a down coat expelling stuffing from a torn arm-seam. "He's cold," Taylor continued. "He's tired. He doesn't feel good. We've got to figure out where he's going to sleep tonight." The boy stared back at them with his big eyes. Thus far they had not heard him speak. "Is that true?" Trip enunciated each syllable as though the kid were deaf and could only read lips. "Are you tired?"

Oriel nodded. With the sleeve of his coat, he swiped quickly at the snot on his upper lip.

"Ugh, don't do that, man," Seth said from up front. He reached in the glove box and rooted around for a Kleenex. "Here, pass that back." Oriel took the tissue and folded it into his palm.

"We probably ought to steer clear of Taylor's for awhile," Brock said, "at least until the heat dies down. Let's crash at Trip's tonight. His mom's probably working."

Trip's house was indeed quiet, his mom at the gym and

his big brother elsewhere, whereabouts unknown, though he'd left little residues of his presence: cologne lingering in the upstairs bathroom, a wet towel on the staircase, a half-eaten Pop-Tart on the kitchen counter. They installed Oriel on the basement futon, though this was Seth's preferred spot. Parenting was about sacrifice. Trip rummaged for some clean sheets and a quilt from the hall closet. Once the child was nestled in his cocoon, sleep seemed to overtake him instantly, and the crew started playing BlackOps 19: KillZone. One by one, as they fell victim to IEDs or knife wounds or M-16 crossfire, the players abandoned the game and staked out spots on various couches or guest beds or sleeping bags in unobtrusive spots. Trip was the last surviving commando. He called in an airstrike on the terrorist stronghold, saved his progress, and turned off the TV, thrusting the basement into pitch-black silence, all the more glaring in the wake of the mortar rounds and flash grenades from a few seconds earlier. Years ago he'd called permanent dibs on the basement couch, so Trip crashed there now, exhausted, still in his clothes. This last mission had taken a toll on him. He had led his troops into an ambush—that's where Brock bit it—and he should've known to expect sniper fire from the burnt-out church where Seth was mortally wounded.

As he was trying to still these thoughts, he heard a strange snuffling sound, wet and rhythmic. The others—even those in far corners of the house who had fallen asleep to the steady discharge of assault rifles—were awakened by it and made their stumbling way toward the source. They turned on a lamp and found Oriel lying on his stomach, breathing noisily, the pillowcase painted with a thick membrane of snot. "Oh, that's sick," Seth said, scratching his head, hair already flat on one side where he'd slept on it.

"I can't listen to that shit," said Taylor. "It's driving me nuts."

"Learn to deal," Brock said. Oriel stirred at the sound of the voices but didn't rise, and the teens stumbled back to their various sleep nests.

It was around three when they were awakened by the cries. Everyone—even Trip's mom, who'd come home from her shift at the gym—rushed to see what was happening. Trip and Brock, who'd been asleep in the basement, bolted upright, flipped on the overhead lights, and were standing now by the futon, staring at Oriel, who stared back at them, eyes wide, breaths short and shallow.

"Who's this?" Trip's mother asked.

"Octave's little brother," Brock responded instantly.

"Who's Octave?"

"A buddy of ours," Brock said. In truth, Mr. Octave was a high school gym teacher who wore tube socks with red piping along the top and school-issue polo shirts tucked into polyester shorts hiked practically to his armpits. There were rumors he'd played Division I back in the Seventies, dropping thirty points in the regional semifinals of the Big Dance. Now his knees were shot and he hobbled around sipping coffee, handing out towels, timing wind sprints with the stopwatch that hung on a lanyard around his neck.

"What's he doing here?" Trip's mother asked.

"His family went on a cruise," Seth said.

Trip's mother regarded Seth skeptically. "And they left him

at home?"

"He's got a cold," Trip said. "They thought the travel would be too much strain, so they asked Brock's parents to babysit. You know how people are always getting sick on those cruise ships."

"Yeah," Brock confirmed, "but my folks are doing line dancing tonight, or something, so they told us to keep an eye on him."

"Jesus, what's that smell?" Taylor said.

"Boys," Trip's mother said, "can't you see he's terrified? He wet the bed."

Having been accused thusly, Oriel clutched the covers around him, trying to hide the evidence. "It was an accident," he said softly. These were the first words they had heard him speak.

"It's fine," Trip's mother said kindly. Then to the others she said, "You're going to have to get him out of those wet clothes and into a hot bath. Trip, there are some old clothes of yours in a storage bin in the laundry room. They'll be too big for him, but at least they'll be clean and dry. You'll have to get those sheets into the wash. You're also going to have to disinfect the futon. There wasn't a rubber sheet down, so I'm sure it soaked through."

"Mom," Trip said, "can you help us?"

She patted her son's head as one might a Great Dane's.

"Not my kid, not my problem. It's late. I'm going to bed." She smiled then, yawned, and departed.

Brock started directing traffic, and they soon had the child bathed and dressed, clean sheets on the futon and the soiled ones in the wash. They were all exhausted by the time they collapsed again in their respective corners.

The sun had barely risen when Trip felt someone tapping his shoulder. Oriel stood before him in baggy borrowed sweatpants, rubbing his dripping nose on the sleeve of one of Trip's old Caliber tees. "Oh, man, don't do that," Trip said. "There's Kleenex in the bathroom."

"At the orphanage we always ate at seven," Oriel said.

"That's cool," Trip murmured, eyes drifting shut.

The boy waited to speak until Trip had fallen asleep again. "It's after seven," he said.

Trip sat up, startled. "Dude, it's Saturday. Chill out."

"But I'm hungry."

Trip sighed. "Look, there's cereal in the kitchen. I think there're some clean bowls in the cupboard. If not, check the dishwasher." Oriel didn't move. "What?" Trip asked finally.

"Where's the kitchen?"

Trip had to accompany him upstairs and sit with Oriel while he ate. He tried engaging the kid in conversation, but Oriel's answers were monosyllabic, a yes or no, sometimes a shrug. Trip wasn't able to glean much information about the boy's background—how he liked the orphanage, how long he'd been there. Oriel wouldn't even open up about hobbies or favorite movies, and Trip began to wonder if the orphans had been exposed to that kind of stuff. He was hesitant to ask about Oriel's parents. Usually the orphans were the result of hurried couplings in cars on Friday nights or too many drinks at one of the clubs downtown. There used to be other solutions to that kind of problem, but the cheap labor had come to be viewed as essential if the US hoped to compete with China in the global economy.

As soon as the others awoke, everyone started playing BlackOps except for Taylor, whose parents had called first thing to tell him about the break-in. They made him come home, there was a police officer who wanted to interview him about the theft, so Oriel took his place on the commando mission. They were raiding a village where a rebel warlord was said to be hiding, but it soon became clear the boy had never played video games before, never touched a controller, and his character kept getting blown up or gunned down, jeopardizing the mission and irritating the other commandos, who were still tired from the previous night's bed-wetting incident.

"Okay, let's do something else," Seth said finally, tossing his controller down, so they wolfed some Doritos and Chips Ahoys before going over to the skate park to teach Oriel the basics. He was given an old cast-off board of Trip's, but they soon found him to be hopelessly uncoordinated. He couldn't even stand on the board without it flying out from under him, leaving Oriel in a crumpled mass on the ground, a surprised look on his face. After awhile he merely sat on a bench watching them on the ramps and railings. By the time they went over to collect him, Oriel was shivering in the brisk autumn air, teeth chattering. They had remembered to patch the holes in his puffy jacket with electrical tape but had not thought to find him gloves or a hat. He held a tissue to his nose, trying to stem the flow of snot, but the Kleenex was insufficient to the task.

"Oh, man," Brock said, "we need to get him home where it's warm." They threw their boards in the back of the minivan and set out for Trip's.

"What are we going to do about school?" Trip asked from the backseat.

"What do you mean?" Seth said.

"Well, don't we have to sign him up, like with Little League? Make sure he's had his shots and all that?"

"No, I think you just put him on the bus when it comes by," Brock said. "They have to take him. It's the law."

"But how will the bus know to stop for him if he's not signed up?" Trip asked.

"They'll see him standing there with his book bag," Brock argued. "It's a no-brainer." The others nodded. And so that issue, at least, was settled.

Back home they started watching some old Pink Floyd concert footage, vintage Roger Waters stuff. Trip noticed Oriel was still shivering so he rounded up a couple blankets for him, but as soon as he had the edges tucked behind the orphan, the way Trip's mother used to do, Oriel struggled to free himself from his blanket-burrito, looking around frantically. Seth glanced up from the TV and noticed the orphan squirming. "What's his deal?" he asked.

"I don't know," Trip said. "Maybe he doesn't like being wrapped up like that. I mean, he never had a mom to tuck him in snug as a bug."

Oriel was taking quick, shallow breaths as he had the night before. Working his arms free, he struggled to stand. "Bathroom," he said.

Trip was pointing in the direction of the little half-bath by the stairs when Oriel put his hand to his mouth, trying but failing to stanch a mist of Dorito-flecked vomit that sprayed forth, settling over the carpet, Brock's Vans, the back of Seth's Stooges t-shirt, the gaming console. A collective cry of horror rang out. Seth clutched at his shirt as though it were some parasitic creature that had latched onto him, his hand coming away slimy. He too started feeling sick and rushed for the bathroom. Brock was running around in circles, stopping periodically to examine his shoes. Trip went to retrieve paper towels and some stain removal spray for the carpet. Oriel, looking much relieved, stood perfectly still, like the calm eye of a storm.

"Maybe you better rest," Brock said, placing his hand on the child's shoulder. This was after he and the others had managed to clean themselves, their clothes, and the basement, and were exhausted by the effort. Thankfully the gaming console still functioned.

"I feel better now, sir," Oriel replied, even managing a wan smile. "What should we play?"

"What do you like?"

"Monopoly."

None of the teens had played in years, but they managed to locate an old Monopoly game and most of the pieces under Trip's bed, and for several hours they trudged around the board, from Mediterranean Avenue to Park Place, in a state of excruciating boredom. At one point, Seth got up for a bag of chips from the pantry but was scolded by Brock.

"Why do you think he hurled?" Brock said. "He's not used to eating all that crap. We need to find something healthy for him. Kids need vegetables." So Seth rooted around in the fridge and came back with carrot sticks and broccoli.

"Can I at least get some ranch to dip them in?" he asked, and Brock nodded. Oriel did seem to enjoy this snack, at least more than the others did. They gnawed at the vegetables half-heartedly. During the game, they again tried talking to Oriel about his past at the orphanage but he seemed utterly focused on the task at hand. Eventually his empire of hotels and railroads was driving the others toward bankruptcy. Seth, down to his last fifty bucks and stuck in jail, didn't even try to extricate himself, despite having a get out of jail free card. Instead he spent three turns incarcerated. Once released, he promptly landed on Virginia Avenue, one of Oriel's hotel properties. He'd already mortgaged his own properties, and when he tried borrowing a couple hundred dollars from Trip, he was informed by the banker—Oriel—that he couldn't.

"This game sucks donkey dick," he said, and they thought for a second Seth was going to upend the board, but he merely left the kitchen table and disappeared downstairs. Soon they heard the familiar sounds of BlackOps.

"I think I'm ready to forfeit," Brock said.

"Yeah, me too," Trip added. "Oriel, you win." The child looked crestfallen but said nothing. He followed them to the basement and sat watching as they played their video game. He was wheezing now and had a rattle in his chest. Probably just a sinus infection, they supposed.

The crew felt they might be pushing their luck to stay at Trip's for another night, so they drove over to Brock's. Brock was the oldest of five siblings and lived in a kid-filled cul-de-sac, so his parents were accustomed to the sight of strange children passing in and out of their house at all hours. That night they put Oriel in a sleeping bag on the floor in Brock's brother's room. Kurt was around the same age as the orphan and they hoped the two might bond, but it wasn't more than half an hour later when Kurt shuffled into the family room, interrupting them in the midst of a BlackOps firefight.

"I can't sleep because of that kid you put in my room," he said. "He's breathing too loud."

Brock abandoned the game so he could relocate Oriel to his room. He hated waking the orphan, who did seem a little under the weather, so he decided to lift him, sleeping bag and all, and carry him. Brock knew Oriel was around Kurt's age from the birth certificate they'd been given at the orphanage, but he was amazed at how much lighter the orphan was than his brother. They were midway down the hall when Oriel woke to find himself being transported through a strange house by a near-stranger toward some unknown destination. The look in his eyes was undiluted panic, and he started freaking out, yelling and flailing. Brock felt something warm and wet soaking through onto his arms and fought the urge to drop Oriel. The kid was like a porcupine or skunk, but his defense mechanism was to piss himself at the slightest whiff of danger.

"For Christ's sake, kid," Brock said, peeling the orphan from the soaked sleeping bag so the two stood facing one another in the hallway.

"Don't tell the others," Oriel said.

"Why not?"

"I don't want them to think I was a bad trade."

"You think we're going to send you back to the orphanage?" Brock asked.

"I'm okay with that," Oriel admitted. "Everyone there was nice. I just don't want to be a disappointment, that's all."

Light from the bathroom slanted across the carpet, illuminating the otherwise darkened hallway. Brock looked up at the framed photos of his family lining one wall. He remembered when they were taken, at the studio out by the mall with the discount packages and the coupon circulars that came in the mail. He recalled the struggle to get everyone bathed and dressed in the formal clothes his mom had ironed and laid out for them the previous night, how frenzied his parents seemed as they worked to knot ties and flatten stray hairs into place, how his dad had been in such a rush to get them to the sitting on time that he almost pulled out in front of a van barreling through an intersection. Yet none of that tension was visible in his parents' faces. In the portraits they appeared happy, relaxed. The constant turmoil had become woven into their lives.

It occurred to Brock that a child might need a family. In PR campaigns, corporations stressed their close ties to the children they adopted. They publicized efforts to educate the children, to set up scholarship funds and athletic programs for them, but Brock questioned the truthfulness of such claims. And he knew that for all the fun he and the others might have with Oriel, all the things they might teach him, they were not a family either, just a loose collective of teens linked by a common interest in skating, psychedelic rock, and low-grade drug use.

The next morning Oriel's cold or sinus infection, whatever

it was, had grown worse. Each breath was labored, and his cheeks were flushed, which the teens mistook for a sign of renewed vigor despite the fact that the child merely curled up on the couch, shivering under a blanket.

Taylor arrived and recounted for them his interview with the police. The cops had been swamped with calls after the football game—altercations, disturbances, vandalism—so were moving quickly from incident to incident, taking little time with issues that could be resolved through an insurance claim. They asked Taylor a few questions about his whereabouts on Friday night and seemed satisfied with his answers. His parents appeared less convinced, and Taylor feared they considered him a suspect. Maybe he was being paranoid, but he felt like his dad studied him the rest of the night for signs of guilt, and his mom—shaken by the break-in—made Taylor and his sister stay home for family time, which meant watching a movie on the smaller 30-inch set Taylor's father had brought up from the basement and planted in the crater left by the missing big-screen.

"Just don't do anything stupid," Brock told him, "and we'll be in the clear."

They wanted to check out the new issues at Comic Haven, but it appeared Oriel was in no condition to travel. After waking briefly, he had again drifted off into a troubled sleep, twisting and jerking, his breathing still ragged. Brock's mother stepped into the family room to invite the boys to breakfast, where a huge stack of blueberry pancakes awaited them. Seeing Oriel on her couch, she went over and pressed the back of her hand to his cheek. "Who is this boy?" she demanded.

"Octave's kid brother," Trip said.

The name didn't ring any bells, which was the point. "Well, whoever he is," Brock's mother said, "you need to take him back to his house. Can't you see how sick he is? The poor thing's running a fever."

This was news to the teens. "Okay, Mom," Brock said. "We will after breakfast."

"No, Brock, right now. This child might need hospitalization."

Her tone startled the boys, as did the word 'hospitalization,' which made them feel as though they'd just swallowed a stone, its cold bulk descending into their stomachs. They conferred in Brock's bedroom.

"What are we going to do?" Trip asked.

"Maybe we could just drop him outside the hospital and take off," Taylor suggested. "I've seen that in movies. The doctors will have to treat him. It's some kind of Hypnotic Oath or something."

"Yeah, and what happens when they trace him back to the orphanage?" Brock asked. If forced to, Brock would've admitted he no longer had much interest in Oriel. After all, he had four siblings of his own, and the barrage of bodily fluids had prevented him from bonding with the child. He was now primarily acting in the interest of self-preservation. "The cops will go question the owner, he'll tell them about the trade for the big-screen, then we're toast."

"Shit," Taylor muttered. "I hadn't thought of that."

"We'll just take him ourselves," Seth said. "The doctor will poke around and prescribe some pills, no big deal."

"Hey, numb-nuts, have you ever been to the doctor? They cost money," Brock said. "Which we don't have."

"When my mom takes me, she just hands the lady at the front desk a card," Trip said.

"That's her insurance card," Brock said, exasperated. "Insurance. Which we also don't have."

"Right, but Trip might be onto something here," Seth said. "All we need is one of those cards. Our folks all have them."

"My mom worked a late shift last night," Trip said, "so she's probably still sleeping. She keeps the card in her purse. It'd be easy enough to swipe."

The walk-in clinics were closed on Sundays, so they had to take Oriel to the ER, which was about as busy as one might expect on a football weekend. The orphan slumped in his chair, fists full of balled-up Kleenexes, while the others thumbed desultorily through magazines detailing celebrity infidelities and addictions, candid photos of stars walking their dogs and buying lattes. The boredom quotient was off the charts.

If the doctor was surprised by the sight of four scraggly-looking skate punks chaperoning a child presenting with obvious symptoms of pneumonia, he didn't show it. He didn't even bother questioning their relationship to the afflicted. The physician was nearing the end of a gruesome 17-hour shift during which he'd seen—among other ailments—a dog bite, a burst appendix, acute alcohol poisoning, a botched suicide by Liquid Drano, and two puncture wounds courtesy of a husband and wife who forked each other over the last of the prime rib on the Bonanza buffet line. The only time he even glanced in the teens' direction was when they protested his recommendation of admitting Oriel for an overnight stay.

"He'd be too scared here by himself," Trip said.

"He'd be more comfortable with his parents," Brock added.

"Whatever," the doctor said, shrugging. He wrote out a prescription for some horse pills and advised them to rent a nebulizer from the medical supply store.

"A what?" Seth said.

"It's a machine to help him breathe."

"Can you write it down for us?" Taylor said. Sighing, the doctor scribbled the word on the back of the script he handed them.

Trip had wisely borrowed his mom's credit card along with the insurance card, so they had money for the pills and the nebulizer. They hustled Oriel up to Seth's bedroom, hoping to avoid any grown-ups. After their run-in that morning with Brock's mom and the puking incident at Trip's, the teens had learned their lesson: parents were to be avoided. And they couldn't risk stepping foot in Taylor's house, which was still sort of a crime scene. They convinced Oriel to take one of the pills without too much difficulty but the nebulizer was another matter. When they plugged it in, it made a sound like an air compressor, and Oriel shied from it like a dog at the vet, shaking his head vehemently and turning his face away when they made overtures of pressing the mask to his face.

"It's for your own good," Trip pleaded, the words sounding uncomfortably like his mother's.

Seth tried reasoning with him. "We wouldn't make you do it unless the doctor said so." But the boy remained unconvinced, and when Brock pinned Oriel's slender arms back so Taylor could hold the mask in place, Brock experienced an unexpected, shameful rush of pleasure. He'd never bullied anyone in his life, yet Brock found that he enjoyed making Oriel do something he didn't want to do. The full weight of the feeling struck him. Those occasions Brock's father had tossed him into the car or held him down and spanked him, the time he forcibly brushed his son's teeth while Brock cried and flailed—had his dad secretly enjoyed them? Did parents relish their little flashes of tyranny? Were they an outlet, some orgasm of pent-up emotion, an expulsion of dangerous waste so the system could reset to more manageable levels? Brock let go of the boy as though he'd been holding his palms to a hot stove, but by that point Oriel had inhaled enough mist to recognize the machine really could make him feel better, and he succumbed to it without further manhandling.

After his nebulizer treatment, the child seemed more comfortable and soon drifted off to sleep while the teens sprawled on the bedroom floor. "Is anyone else starting to think this was a bad idea?" Taylor whispered.

"Which part?" Seth asked.

"All of it. I mean, our weekend is shot and we didn't do anything cool. It was all just cleaning and hard work. And this kid is practically a mute."

"It'll take time," Trip said.

"That's the thing," Brock said. "He's ours now. Forever." This word frightened the crew, who like other teens were extremely shortsighted, the future hovering far in the distance, inky and ill-defined. They couldn't imagine being twenty, let alone forty or fifty, possessing something that would outlive them.

"We signed papers," Taylor agreed.

"I don't think you can enter into a binding contract with a minor," Seth said. His mom's last boyfriend had been an attorney, so Seth's observations on legal matters were given added weight.

"Let's just get him onto the bus in the morning and we'll take it from there," Brock said.

They were right to assume the bus driver would stop for Oriel. The driver, a retiree of the plumber's and steamfitter's local, was merely counting the days until he could quit this crummy part-time gig and escape to Vero Beach. If he saw a kid waiting, he picked him up, no questions asked. He wasn't about to get canned for leaving some student out in the cold to freeze like that driver over in Harkness had done.

The confusion didn't begin until Oriel got to school. He filed off the bus with the other kids, but while they hung up coats and backpacks and grabbed folders and notebooks from their lockers, Oriel roamed the hallways. He was wearing new jeans and a new button-down shirt, his sneakers bright white. His jacket still had that polyester-perfume store smell about it. His backpack, also new, contained packs of pencils and erasers, glue sticks, notebooks, Kleenex, a few comics, half a pack of bubblegum, and Seth's sister's old MP3 player preloaded with Britney Spears and techno-pop. Oriel felt that if he kept walking, people would assume he knew where he was headed and would ignore him, but as the hallways emptied his presence became more noticeable. The bell rang, startling the orphan, who had never set foot in a school before. His previous lessons had always been conducted at the orphanage.

It was the librarian who finally stopped him. When she found he could not answer the most basic questions about his teacher, his classroom, or the location of his locker, she guided him to the office, where Oriel sat digging in his pack for a tissue, nose running, feverish face flushed from all that walking.

The principal was somewhat flustered to find a strange child in his midst. After his secretary failed to find evidence of the boy's name in the school rolls, Principal Hargrove led Oriel into his office. "Son," he said kindly, "I'm not sure you're at the right place. Can you tell me your mom and dad's name so I can give them a call?"

"I don't have a mom or dad," Oriel said softly.

"Everyone has a mom and a dad," the principal explained. "That's just a biological fact."

"No, I mean I don't know who they are."

"You're an orphan?" This too caught Principal Hargrove off guard. "From which orphanage?"

"Mr. Forsythe's."

"On County Line or downtown?"

"1263 County Line Road," Oriel recited.

"How'd you escape?"

"I didn't," the boy said, a little affronted. "I was adopted."

"Oh, okay." Principal Hargrove smiled broadly to indicate some great confusion had been resolved. "Well, just tell me who your adoptive parents are and I'll give them a quick call."

Here Oriel faltered. The teens, for all their constant chatter, had never bothered to introduce themselves. He began chewing a hangnail. "One's called Trip, I think, and there's a Seth…and a

Brad, maybe. I'm not sure of the other one's name."

"Son, you're going to have to take that hand away from your mouth. I can't make out what you're saying."

Oriel repeated the names as he remembered them.

"Kiddo," the principal said once he'd finished, "only two parents to a child, that's generally how it works." Mr. Hargrove leaned back in his chair and stared out the window at the gunmetal sky. The flag was whipping back and forth, prompted by a strong north wind, the last of the autumn leaves swirling and eddying, coming to rest along the curb where the busses parked. He tapped a fountain pen on his lower lip and could taste the acrid ink on his tongue. He wondered if his lip was blue. "Did you say Trip and Seth?" he asked suddenly.

The boy nodded.

Principal Hargrove began to recall a quartet of boys who passed through his halls a few years back. They had been students of middling merit, borderline delinquents, causing turmoil in the classroom, pulling pranks in the music and art rooms. In the gymnasium, where tables were arranged each day for lunch, the boys had bent silverware and tossed Jell-O at the high gym ceiling to see if it would stick. (It did, and Hargrove was forced to hire a contractor to scrape and repaint, not to mention revising the whole lunch menu to eliminate any foods that might double as bonding agents.) Yes, he remembered now. These boys had routinely blessed the girls with window-rattling bursts of flatulence fueled by a steady diet of Ding-Dongs and Mountain Dew. They had stolen petty objects from their homes to sell on the playground, items like powerlifting gloves and swimsuit catalogs the other kids paid good money for. Anyone they disapproved of they called a homo-tard. Many over the years had earned this appellation, so many in fact that Hargrove came to picture them as some species of early man, walking upright but with hairy knuckles dragging. To his chagrin, the word survived its creators and could still be heard knocking around the school.

By sixth grade the boys were coming to class reeking of pot and spanking it to girlie mags in the staff bathroom, which was lockable. One Halloween a miscreant spray-painted a giant neon cock-and-balls on the side of the school. Hargrove knew who it was but lacked the evidence to prosecute. Seth Grady and Trip Winton. The third was not named Brad, but Brock. Brock Anderton. And the fourth was Taylor Evans. What could they possibly have to do with this whole mix-up?

Hargrove called the orphanage but the man who answered was cagey with him, citing confidentiality, feigning ignorance—a dead end—so the principal started dialing parents. Meanwhile the orphan sat before him looking miserable, snot issuing from him at an alarming clip, and the principal tossed a box of Kleenex to Oriel while waiting for someone to pick up. Hargrove seemed to recall that of the four households, Brock's was the only one still intact, but when he got the Andertons' machine he moved on to Trip's mother.

"Yes?" she answered groggily, coming off another late shift at the gym. The principal stated his reason for calling and asked if she was aware of what by now he had deemed The Oriel Situation.

"The what?" Trip's mother said.

"There's a boy in my office," Principal Hargrove repeated,

"and I don't know where he came from, but he claims your son and some of his friends adopted him from a local orphanage."

"I don't think that's possible," Trip's mother murmured, and the principal thanked her for her time, about to hang up. "Wait," she added, more alert now. "There was a kid hanging around this weekend, a younger boy, kind of sickly. They said he was somebody's kid brother. That could've been him."

After the call ended, Trip's mother lay in bed, mind racing. She loved her son and his friends, but sometimes they could be such jackasses. The first thing she needed to do was check her bank balance and credit card statements, a lesson she'd learned after unwittingly bankrolling Pearl Jam tickets and a near mint X-Men inaugural issue. Sure enough, when she went online she found suspicious charges for Gaddis Memorial, CVS, Abercrombie, Foot Locker, American Eagle. From these it was easy enough to chart the crew's whereabouts. They had gone to the emergency room for some reason and afterward filled a prescription. Then they went clothes shopping at the mall—whether for themselves or the boy she couldn't be sure.

The charge from Gaddis was a co-pay, and Debbie hoped it was Trip who had required the medical attention. If someone else had been treated on her insurance card, she'd probably get stuck with the full bill. Wait, was she actually wishing injury on her own son? Sudden fear for his wellbeing stabbed at her, and Debbie grabbed her coat and purse and left for the high school, not even bothering with her hair and makeup.

Normally Trip would've welcomed a break from geometry, but it was ominous to receive a summons to the office on a Monday morning from one of the school secretaries. The hallways were empty, the floors still buffed to a high shine where the weekend cleaning crew had gone over them. Trip noticed a sheet of paper on the floor with a dusty shoeprint on it, and when he stepped closer he saw it was Rick Shoenfeld's English homework. Rick Shoenfeld was on the swim team. He had thick casing-like legs and terrible eyesight and smelled of pool chemicals. A couple years back he made the mistake of trusting his only friend, Peter Melton, with the terrible secret that he sometimes enjoyed coating his genitals with Cool Whip and allowing the family dog to lick it off. He was promptly exposed, a betrayal that moved Peter Melton a rung or two up the social ladder and caused Rick, forever after, to be known as Whip-Dick. Trip left the paper where it lay.

The outer office was walled in a sort of semi-opaque reinforced glass so Trip could only make out shadows within, but as he and the secretary drew closer Trip saw his mom leaning on the front desk, talking to the vice-principal, her hair matted flat on one side where she'd slept on it. She was still wearing her work shirt with the gym logo on it, and she'd thrown a skirt over some workout tights. "Oh, shit," Trip muttered. The secretary regarded him but said nothing, figuring profanity was the least of his problems. The vice-principal's office was brick and windowless like some kind of holding cell. Bryce Haverford had tried to make it over into a shrine of his accomplishments, framed diplomas on the walls along with less impressive unframed certificates memorializing the completion of trainings, online modules, and CPR certifications. Vice-Principal Haverford had a Dare to Be Drug Free poster above his desk, and a letter, circa 2015, thanking him for his service as a Kidtastic Klass Klown. Trip had not heard of the organization and wondered if the credential had been produced on Haverford's office printer.

It did not take long to break him. They started with the credit card charges, working their way backwards until Trip finally confessed that he and his friends had stolen the big-screen from Taylor's parents, swapping it for a young boy. "We weren't really thinking," Trip admitted. The inarguable logic of this left the others stunned.

Vice-Principal Haverford knew enough about the four teens to conclude they were probably the worst caregivers imaginable for an impressionable child. He had to struggle to come up with a worse option: some Hell's Angels, maybe, or some tweakers or Neo-Nazis. "Jeeze," he said, leaning back in his chair, putting his hands behind his head and gazing up at the ceiling. "I'm not sure this is a school matter." Trip and his mother waited for the vice-principal to say more. "I'm not sure it even needs to be a police matter," he added, "assuming Taylor's folks decide not to press charges over the TV. To be honest, I'm not sure what kind of matter this is. That might be for you all to decide. I just hope you get that kid back where he belongs."

Mr. Haverford called the other teens out of class, and as soon as they saw Trip standing outside the office with his mom they knew what was up. They were made to call their parents, who met them at the school, and they formed a four-car caravan over to the elementary to pick up Oriel, who was waiting for them in the principal's office.

As she drove, Trip's mother glanced over now and again

at her son. She was mad about the theft of her credit card and the Evans's big-screen, but more than anything she was baffled. Of all the things they could've traded the TV for, all the things other teens would've traded it for—drugs, cigarettes, video games, comic books, hand-jobs at the Asian massage parlor—they chose a child. Even if meant with the best of intentions it was still a tad sick and wrong. "What were you going to do with him?" she asked.

Trip looked at her, surprised. "We were going to raise him."

"Trip," and here Debbie found herself unaccountably on the verge of tears, "what do any of you know about raising a child?"

"We were learning."

"What did you learn?"

"Well, for one thing you have to dress them warm. A hat and gloves. And you have to find them their own space where they feel comfortable." He thought for a second. "And you have to give them healthy stuff to eat, not just junk food. And you have to take them to the doctor right away if they get sick, and sometimes you have to do shit with them you don't really want to do, like boring kid games."

Now Debbie did cry a little, though smiling, as she reached over and tousled her son's hair. It was true he had learned a few lessons, had in fact picked up on this parenting thing more quickly than she ever did. But then, she was never the most attentive student.

When faced with this crowd of angry parents, Mr. Forsythe didn't put up much resistance, especially when Oriel came running in and attached himself to the man's leg. He had to admit he missed the little bugger and regretted his decision to ship him off with a Dodge Caravan full of teenaged punks in the first place. Forsythe could see that Oriel was no worse for wear, though his sinus troubles had perhaps been amplified by the change of setting. Taylor's parents sought out their big-screen and found a whole herd of young children clustered around it as Big Bird and Oscar the Grouch burst forth in full splendor. Taylor's dad was about to unplug the set when Taylor's mom placed her hand on his forearm. "Let's think about this for a second," she said, looking upon the shining faces of the children. "We could donate the TV to the orphanage, then Taylor and his friends could work to buy us a new one, a bigger one. It's a win-win. The orphans get to keep their TV and we get a new one, plus a tax write-off."

"What about the boys?" Taylor's dad asked, releasing the plug. "What do they get out of it?"

"I didn't say it was a win-win-win," Taylor's mom said, smiling. "But they'll learn a valuable lesson."

"That's definitely worth something," Taylor's dad agreed. "Character building."

"Yes, character building," Taylor's mom said, and there was a touch of cruelty in their laughter.

Only the matter of the paperwork remained, so Brock handed back Oriel's birth certificate and the copies of the legal forms they had signed. Mr. Forsythe placed the certificate in his file drawer and shredded everything else. Seth ran out to the van and returned with the old skateboard they had lent for Oriel's use.

"Here you go, little man," he said, thrusting the board at Oriel. "You better practice so you can show us some tricks when we come back."

The child beamed. "You're coming back?"

"Definitely," Brock said, stepping forward and patting the child on the head. Trip and Taylor also came forward to pat Oriel's back and give him high fives.

And they did return regularly all through the winter and into the spring, and when summer came, Mr. Forsythe's assistant, Harry, would chaperone them over to the neighboring orphanage with its mammoth parking lot, perfect for practicing skateboard basics, and they even got Harry onto the board once or twice, he of the western shirts and jeans and cowboy boots, cigarette dangling from his mouth like the Marlboro Man of old. But one Saturday in September when they arrived with some new comics for Oriel, Harry shook his head from his post behind the front desk and said, "He's gone," and they weren't sure at first what that meant, thinking maybe he'd simply been taken on some sort of field trip or medical check-up, but then Harry added, "adopted."

The feeling of loss came suddenly over them, a sensation so stinging and so foreign they kept their eyes focused on the floor tiles and could not risk meeting one another's eyes. To see the emotion pooling there would've been shameful—not as bad as dipping your balls in dessert topping and having a canine lap at them, but shameful nevertheless. Eventually the feeling grew more familiar to them as they split with girlfriends or were distanced from one another by jobs or junior college or, in one case, the armed forces, but they never felt it as keenly as they did that afternoon. When you're sixteen, you firmly believe that everything and everyone is fixed in place, and the concept of endings is one that no one bothers explaining to you because, hey, why spoil the party?

"He wasn't bought by one of those corporations, was he?" Trip said, jaw clenched, staring Harry in the eye, and Harry knew how he felt, he really did.

"No, he was adopted by a real nice man and lady looking to start a family," Harry lied.

CRICK

Fourth of July and the smell of cigarettes and beer breath passing between Dad and Uncle Jack is almost as thick as park dogs, onions, and jet fuel from the B-52's and Firebird's tearing up the afternoon sky. Kids are running kites, mock-up model planes held above their heads, and they're laughing. All over the park, tailgates are dropped. Tents sag. Bonfires burn bright even in the sunlight. It's the same every year: Dad and Uncle Jack dragging us kids out for fireworks, and we're driving snail's pace through Winnebagos and minivans looking for a spot to park—seven of us in the truck.

"You boys wake up," Dad says and spits out his window.

"I'm up," I say, more adult than my brother Dynamo, who's eight, wiping half-crusted drool from his chin, whining, "Can we eat'r sandwiches? I'm hungry."

I wish I hadn't argued for shotgun. I'm wedged in the front seat with Dynamo, Dad, and Uncle Jack, whose hot arm is sliding sweaty across my neck. In the truck bed are Uncle Jack's kids: Cousin Libby, the oldest at fifteen, and twins Blake and Riley—the babies, we call them, though they're the same age as Dynamo. Only link between us is the window behind my head, though in the rearview mirror, I can see Libby by the tailgate, her auburn head blinking in and out of sight as she flicks the twins in their ears to wake them. Her eyes are the same chilly gray as Uncle Jack's, and twice, on the drive up, she caught me looking.

Uncle Jack nudges Dynamo. "You quit crying if you get a sandwich?"

"Not crying," Dynamo huffs.

"Shut up, Sideways," I say, calling him the nickname that he hates, that Dad leans over and knocks me in the head for using, that people dreamed up after Dynamo started walking because he's got one leg longer than the other—bends him sideways when he stands. But Dad says, *Kid was born sideways for a reason. God cooked him that way.*

Dynamo likes that. "God cooked me sideways," he rattles off in the truck cab. Then—when offered—declines his sandwich.

"Boys got too much hungry in you," Dad says. "Our house, we didn't ask for food. We went out and found it."

"Bobby did," Uncle Jack says.

"Bobby did," Dad agrees, as we pass what looks to me like the perfect spot to park.

Uncle Bobby was the eldest of the three. Helicopter pilot in Vietnam—he never made it home. Now it's the Cameron County air show every Fourth of July. Dad and Uncle Jack and all of us cousins sardined in the truck so that later we can watch the Black Diamond jets, the Iron Eagles, biplanes and Blue Angels flipping, diving, and we'll cheer for them, we'll chase them—like we're cheering and chasing after Uncle Bobby in the Cameron sky.

But this year's different.

This year Dad and Uncle Jack are searching for Bradley Coleman's trailer, stripe up the center with a sun catcher sprawled out for shade. Uncle Jack says they have to do what lawboys won't. No registered child molester's living in Cameron County—not near Darrel and Jack Gibson's kids. Says him and Dad grew up stupid and brawling, slaughtered pigs five years on Kerber's Farm. They'd seen blood before.

"Pass me a punk," Dad says, and I hand him another Genesee. He's drunk, I know, blood-stained eyes looking pink. He's

excited, and I am, too—for the air show, and for finding Coleman's
trailer, catching a glimpse of him: a child molester. But it's hard to
say what Dad and Uncle Jack expect to do. Dad's thicker now, and
fat. He's not the Darrel Gibson of the stories I've heard, the man
who fought six bikers with an axe handle outside Cooper's garage.
Mostly, he's a good, harmless man. At least until he's drinking with
Uncle Jack—the iron jaw and mustache, the silvery-gray eyes and
bulletproof cheeks. Those two drunk together and they'll be spark-
ing M-80s, blowing up bushes, catching tires and logs on fire with
gas Uncle Jack siphoned-sucked from the truck, laughing gasoline-
teethed and spitting in the grass.

For all I know, they could kill the man.

I even overheard Aunt Patty telling Mom once that when
Uncle Bobby was still alive, he, Dad, and Uncle Jack found
Grandma Gibson beaten in the kitchen—her bloody leg against
the counter, sunlight spilling over the stainless sink. She was nearly
hidden in the shade. The three of them carried her into the living
room. They couldn't have been more than kids themselves. Took
time, but eventually she admitted Sam Pearson, the neighbor and
Granddad Gibson's best friend, came in drunk trying to kiss her.
She tried to stop him and he raped her. She made them swear not
to tell. Said Granddad would love her different after that.

So the brothers kept the secret. Waited near a month and
took Sam Pearson fishing up the Susquehanna River. Sam told
stories the whole ride out, kept throwing his arm around their
shoulders, telling them he loved them like sons. He thanked them
for bringing him. They took a boat and a cooler full of beer out at
dawn and smoked cigarettes fishing while the fog rolled upstream,

surrounding them. Time came, it was Uncle Bobby that did what needed done, and he used a knife. Uncle Jack held the long-barrel twenty-two to Sam's head and made him swear not to scream.

"How about the time he came home with peaches?" Uncle Jack says, recalling still, the stories of Uncle Bobby.

"Took them from Old Lady Warren," Dad remembers.

"Sonofabitch climbing through our bedroom window. I swear to God he fucked her for them." And they laugh a minute as we bang over mole holes and rocks toward Keister Creek, where we've parked before. I can see a rope swing swaying from a tree, gathering sunlight in its thread, water cool and shimmering beneath it.

"These assholes," Uncle Jack says, pointing off near the tree to a group of teen-aged boys all bare-chested and flexing by the creek, army shorts dark with water. A group of pretty girls are sitting smoking cigarettes in bathing suits on a shelf-rock bench. "Dreaming hard for that seventeen-year-old ass."

"Dream on!" Dad shouts out the window, nudging me, and smiling. The boys throw up double fists triumphantly, as if he'd complimented them. I slide down the seat, hoping the girls that turn to look can't see me squeezed between him and Dynamo, who's sitting straight up smiling at them, yelling, too, for them to "Dream on!" until I pinch his ribs and he smacks my hand, asking, "Uncle Bobby shoot them hills with napalm in the war?"

"He did what they asked him," Dad says. A bead of sweat drips from his clean-shaved face to my shoulder. He's hitting the breaks, dropping the truck loud into reverse, and all of us are bouncing back and forth as the gears shift.

"First Christmas home," Uncle Jack says, flicks his cigarette out, and mats his mustache against his sweaty lip. "We were out back in Pappy's shed getting stoned and leaning over the kerosene heater to keep warm from the snow coming through the window. I asked Bobby if he fucked any cunt over there, or if he'd least gotten his dick sucked good the way my buddies home on leave said they got. So he goes all serious all the sudden, says they were off near the edge of the FOB when he heard a whisper in the bushes. Almost pulled the trigger and started shooting 'till he saw a girl's face poking out, dirty, and shy as a turtle in a shell. Said he swore to God he'd known her all his life. Girl couldn't be more than fourteen years old."

And just as Dad is clutching, revving the truck engine to keep it running, and the creek is so close I can smell it, and I'm waiting to find out what Uncle Bobby did with the girl, Libby pokes her head in from the back window. "I'm getting out."

"Like Hell," Uncle Jack says. "Wearing those tiny shorts like your old man can't buy you jeans; I'll have to kill someone today."

"Please, daddy." Her voice is a warm breath on my neck. "There's Becky Johnson and the girls over by the swing." In the mirror, I can see her bony shoulder sun-burned and bending from her tank top, sun gathering on her skin. I have to close my eyes. Even at fifteen, she feels so much older than me.

"Go on," Dad says. "Let her go." He winks, and Libby jumps out before Uncle Jack can protest. She's running toward the rope swing waving to her friends, and I need to get out, too. I can climb over Dynamo, through the window.

"I'm getting out," I say the same way Libby did.

"Like Hell," Dad says. "Someone's got to help unload the cooler." Which is annoying, since Dad is going to unload the cooler himself, and Uncle Jack will set up the chairs and grill, insisting there's a certain way to do it.

Then through Dad's window, I see Libby take Becky in her arms. The bare-chested boys stand watching, looking hungry. Behind them, venders man tables spilling with model planes and learner's kits for sale, and old men are drunk, wearing American-flag shirts talking through mustaches and hotdogs. People lean heavily on the fence near the fuel yard, happy to see the jets being gassed up, Angels and Eagles glowing under pilot's wax. From the Flyboys Youth hanger, the sound of rivet guns snap, drills zip, and kids are sanding, sawing. And later, when Dynamo begs for the arts& crafts festival, I'll drop him off and join the guys my age for flying remote-control planes, but right now, it's Libby—her gray eyes peering back over her shoulder, waving. Uncle Jack leaning out his window, yelling, "I see you, fuckers." To the teen-aged boys. "I'll be here all night."

"Can we swim in the crick," Dynamo asks, wide awake now.

"Swim where?" Uncle Jack asks, and for the first time, he and Dad catch eyes and laugh. Dad nearly splashes the dashboard with a mouthful of Genesee.

"In the crick," Dynamo smiles, as if he's in on the joke. "I want to swim, too." He makes a stupid face, his big-assed eyes the size of half dollars all blue and looking to me to laugh with him. Sometimes I swear we can't be brothers. He doesn't even know they're laughing because a crick's what Dad and Uncle Jack call a man with no dick. Started on Kerber's Farm, cutting pig's dicks off for cooking.

"Only one crick here," Uncle Jack says as we back into a spot, and all our heads turn at once, it seems, toward Coleman's striped trailer, him sitting in a lawn chair out front.

When we're parked, we pour from the truck. The day is fat with humidity—the smell of jet wax and creek water as thick as smoke. Dynamo and the twins eat their sandwiches on the tailgate, and Uncle Jack doesn't stop watching Coleman's trailer. Even when Coleman's gone, Uncle Jack is searching, his face like a sniper's, cold and patient. And Dad naps off his buzz in the shade by the truck tire.

Downstream, I can see Libby with her friends, half-submerged in the creek. They've stripped down to swim suits, piled their tee-shirts and shorts in the grass. I'm bending around the side of the truck to peep their skinny backs and sun-wet legs flexed as they trudge through the water. All the girls my age are too young to have bodies like that, with the exception of Gabby Wells, who wore nothing but a tank top once in the fifth grade and her chest bounced around all afternoon and there wasn't one of us boys, I swear God, that didn't go home and didn't think about it from under the blankets of our bunk beds that night.

Now the announcer's voice is a mechanic throb through the park. Firebird formation's prepping to kick off the show, the sound of engines rolling across the field, and Libby and the girls are drifting from my sight.

A few lots down, the Pitbull Pen's a barking spectacle—near fifty of them. Enough to draw me to it.

Their owners bring them every year for the Pitbull show the same weekend as the air event. They call it "show," as if they're giving prizes for lookers, but they're an ugly bunch—not a single dog pretty enough to show: mouths dripping wet with foam and drool, some scar-faced and one-eyed. They got blotchy skin and mange. Bunch of monsters bathed in dog shit and piss. Rumor is: once the jet lovers leave, and the air show clears, pilots pulling planes out on eighteen-wheelers, people say the dog fighting starts. It's a smaller, more vicious crowd, too—guys with long hair and skull shirts who flip us the finger when we pass.

The dogs are on the edge of the field, by the woods, enclosed by a poorly constructed chicken-wire fence near six-feet tall. Mostly, they're separated by short chains and leashes, but some owners bring more than one, whole packs—small, sharp-toothed ones kept away from the tall, muscular ones. Sometimes, the chicken wire bends so hard, it nearly snaps. Dogs dig holes, try to escape, and eventually, there's so much mud and dirt it's half pit, half pen. Every time the announcer's microphone screeches, the dogs howl. They bark. They cry. Some kids kick the fence, but mostly, we ignore the sound of their barking. We understand that they're separate from us plane-engine boys.

"I hate those dogs," Dynamo says from the tailgate, mouthful of turkey sandwich. "I'd like to jump in that pen and give 'em a kick."

The twins cheer simultaneously, but Blake says, "Let's go! I'll jump in with you!"

"The Hell you will," Uncle Jack says. "You'll end up like Ronnie Sherer's boy," talking about the great remembered incident of ten years ago: 1971.

"You saw him?" Dynamo asks, and the twins chime in. "Yeah, you saw him? You saw the boy? Wish we saw him." Though we've grown used to the sound of the dogs, none of us has forgotten the story.

"Don't go wishing for things you don't understand," Uncle Jack says. "That boy went missing and they recruited Uncle Darrell and me. Needed experience in the pen. The kid's own daddy was crying like a child on his knees. Those dogs left the kid stinking in the dark."

"Where'd you find him?" I ask. By now, Libby's gone somewhere downstream with her friends and the six of us are stuck keeping eyes on Bradley Coleman's empty trailer.

"Middle of the field," Dad says. As if to give truth to the story, he sits up, voice groggy from his nap. He turns his baseball cap backwards on his head. "They say he snuck 'round back of the pen, rattled that fence and agitated the dogs. They dragged him through a hole they dug and bit his voice box out his throat. No one heard him scream. Chewed his face so bad they had to tell it was him by the ring on his hand."

Dynamo and the twins are busting up laughing already, slipping away from the story to watch some kid's remote-control plane by the creek, less interested than me. "Kid live?" I ask.

"Dead," Uncle Jack says, cracking another Genesee. "Family sued the park, so they put six suspicious dogs down. Lined them up and shot them each in the head. People feel better about that."

When the Firebirds finish, the national anthem scratches through the speakers, crashing into its own echo as the Eagle Team takes the clear-blue sky, and Dad and Uncle Jack have gone from watching Coleman to taunting him. They throw cans at him. They tell him to keep his eyes where they belong or they'll cut his tongue out his mouth. Uncle Jack pisses on Coleman's lawn chair when he's inside the trailer, and they laugh.

There's something about Coleman that is sad to me. He's a clean-shaved man. His eyes are round and green. When he walks, he digs his hands way into his pockets as if he's reaching for money, or a lucky penny. When Dad and Uncle Jack chuck beers at him, some empty, some—by the gunshot smack they make against the side of Coleman's trailer— even full, he only turns his head, and scuttles like some possum back into the quiet darkness of his trailer.

I wonder if Dad or Uncle Jack is capable of the violence their stories promise. I wonder, if Uncle Bobby was around, alive and growing fat and drunk with them, if he'd be taunting too. Or if he'd be prepping some silver chopper for flight, the main attraction of the show, Cameron County's own Bobby Gibson—war hero, fearless—and all of us, even Dad and Uncle Jack, would be too busy chasing after the sight of him above to be watching out for Coleman. I wonder if, now I'm sipping Dad's Genesee, and Dynamo and the twins are running somewhere with the neighbor kids, and Libby's back—lying in the truck bed, her shirt rolled over her shoulders, jean shorts unbuttoned and showing her bathing suit bright yellow, her pale skin pinking under the sun—if I should lie down next to her sharing sips of Dad's beer, or if I should be too worried for Coleman, and the punishment that awaits him.

"You never said what happened," I interrupt Dad and Uncle Jack from their whispering near the cooler. I burp, holding the beer can in the air so they'd see me and take it. I'm thinking suddenly of *cunt*, the sound of it stuck rolling on my tongue since Uncle Jack's story. "With Uncle Bobby. That girl in the bush."

"Brought her back to the FOB," Dad says, picking the story up, walking back as if maybe he'd give up the cause and join us, and the show. "And he hid her by his bunk. But she was bleeding. Must've caught some shrapnel in the leg. Cut her good. Said he kept wiping it, trying to soak the shit up with a shirt, but it kept coming. Black like tar, and thick, too."

But the sound of Coleman's screen door slamming turns our heads. Even Libby sits up. He's leaving this time in a hurry, looking over his shoulder. Dad and Uncle Jack jog off tossing beers, stumbling as they flip him the finger and laugh, like they plan to steal his food like bullies.

Libby goes, too—into the thick of the park, disappearing. Annoyed maybe, or bored.

Some years, I'm all over the park. I'll walk off watching an F-16 formation spiraling so hard I'm convinced it's losing control, that it's about to crash the woods beside the interstate, and suddenly I've walked half a mile from the truck. So many people crowded. So much noise and smoke. But this year, I'm more aware of the time between air shows, of the announcer trying to rev us up, the distance I've gained from our truck and the cousins, of Dynamo tailing beside me—a gnat stuck to sweaty skin. Every time I have Libby in my sights, when she's leaned back, for instance, against the truck drinking pop, or she's building a fan from a plastic cup watching the show, and I'm sort of following her getting brave enough to say something, Dynamo's there stepping on my toes. I can't even pawn him off on arts & crafts. He's all, *Gary, wait up*, and, *Check this trailer out*, or, *You ever think of flying, Gary*.

And we're hardly half the perimeter when a boy on a 50cc motorcycle rides past and bites it by the dog pens.

"Dusted!" Dynamo shouts and darts over trying to crowbar the bike from the ground. The throttle's dug into dirt, revving the two-stroke to a scream. Behind Dynamo, the pitbulls attack the fence, their teeth a brutal, slobbery shine snatching at his shirt.

"Have to lift the goddamned thing," I say, shoving against the fence. I lift the bike off the kid, who rides off with his smoky exhaust clouding a three-rail trailer. But Dynamo is startled by the dogs a neck's snap from his cut-sleeve shirt, his jean shorts and un-tied army boots too large for his feet, and he's running back toward the truck, toward Dad and Uncle Jack and the twins. Short leg lifting, dropping. Head tilted sideways. Stupid kid, I swear to God.

At dusk, only the real air fans are lingering. Trash is left burning in hundred-gallon cans. The smell of bonfire and burger grease is stuck on everything; your hair, your clothes. Before us, there's wide open field and muddy children. Dynamo and the twins are laugh-ing on the grass with a group of kids waiting for the final air event before the fireworks: the F6F Hellcat—all chrome, Henry Hobson in the pilot's seat. Just when the air is cooling, and crickets singing he'll fire over the horizon, chrome catching moonlight and trailers and blinking in the sky.

This time last year, Libby and I were in the Vanderbelt's tent talking shit on the show. The Vanderbelts left to watch and we were alone. We'd spent most the night playing stupid board games, talking. Ashley Vanderbelt said a girl at school gave a guy head in the bathroom. I was lying on my stomach, and while Ashley described how the girl put his dick in her mouth by the sinks, my elbow brushed Libby's. I felt myself get hard. I crept toward her, so slightly it seemed it took an hour to move an inch. But somehow, I'd moved my hand to her back. She let my fingertips rest there. I'd been hard, it seemed, all night. Terrified she'd discover it, I pressed my hips into the grass beneath the tent, hand on Libby's skin. I pushed my pinky down the back of her pants, just enough that I had it resting in the top of her crack and I was shaking as Henry Hobson roared into the sky outside and the park cheered and I came in my pants. Felt dizzy, then sick—nearly threw up. Snatched my hand back and left the tent.

Now, by the truck, Dad and Uncle Jack are so drunk they're holding each other steady. Couple buddies with them are drinking the last of the Genesee from the cooler. Cigarette butts are sprinkled by the tires. The smell of urine starts to penetrate the night—all those drunks pissing in the grass at once. Hobson is flipping his chrome bird in the moonlit sky and Dynamo is running crooked after the sound of the Hellcat's engine, disappearing over the hill toward the creek. I don't think I've ever seen the boy so in love with anything in his life.

I want to find Libby, talk to her this night in the dark, but again, she's gone with her girls. I can't help feeling sick and excited when I think of it, of last summer, of being alone with her again. I hate it, and myself. Even the twins, who look like her. I hate them. And Uncle Jack, his gray eyes. I hate him. This truck bed, all uncomfortable and rusted. I hate it. And there's a light on in Coleman's trailer blurring the stars above it. The glow is spilling out into the field, lighting up the side of our truck, empty beer cans gleaming in the grass.

Fireworks are the kicker, and we've waited all night for them. For twenty minutes, the park bleeds purple and blue, red, yellow, and green. Air stinks like gunpowder as the reverb pounds the fields like thunder. Then: the best part. Just when the finale seems as good as it gets, and Dad's rebel yelling, high-fiving Uncle Jack, a Stealth Bomber will blast through the night sky, carrying with it the wind and leaves, the scent of river water and summer. And the whole damn park will become one giant fucking hard-on of chanting.

Across the field, women holding babies are standing on the roofs of Winnebagos. Young girls and boys are lying over windshields eating red, white, and blue snow cones and now-stale popcorn from the Flyboys Hanger. And there's Libby, a hundred feet away hunched under a trailer umbrella kissing some older boy with army shorts and exercised arms. He's grabbing her ass and Uncle is Jack moving toward them. The boy bails, disappears somewhere into still-parked trailers and trucks. Uncle Jack and Libby are faced off with each other, arguing, but their voices are lost when the show begins, the first explosion lighting up the sky.

There's a collective and surprisingly dull cheer spreading as Uncle Jack yells at Libby. She turns and he trips trying to make her hear him. It's the first time I've ever seen him look so pathetic, though that's not the word that comes to me. No one knows where Dynamo is and no one cares. I sure as Hell don't. I want to run to the edge of the creek to where we flew remote-control planes and threw Frisbees. I want to find my air-show friends, the same guys I see every year, and talk shit to them, cuss to them, say *cunt* to them like I understand what it means and spit between drags of their fathers' cigarettes. I want to stand in the middle of the jet field while engines cool, and there's a magic still in the fumes hanging in the air. But Dad grabs hold of my shoulder, spins me toward him. His voice is scratched from cheering, and he's drunk. I hear his confusion of whatever it is he thinks I'm feeling standing there watching the fireworks alone when he says, "You're about a man now, Gary. You're old enough to know this."

He sits me down on an empty lawn chair near the truck. "So don't be a stupid ass telling no one. Get us put in jail. All of us—even you. Don't go fucking up."

When Dad and Uncle Jack found out Coleman was registered, they asked their boys at the station about running him out of Cameron. Coleman had served his time, though—three years. He'd moved into Cameron from Harrisburg and was allowed to live his life, quietly. People needed to respect that.

Dad was picking plums at the grocery store a few months later when Coleman strolled up next to him. He started picking plums, too, as if he belonged there, as if he'd gone and committed his crime and now, since he'd served for it, he was some kind of free man.

"Hate a bad plum," he said, smiling at dad.

Caught off guard, Dad smiled back, and left. He sat in the parking lot for nearly an hour, unable to start the truck and watching people leave the store, feeling ashamed, as if sharing a smile over plums had somehow made him guilty, too. He said it haunted him. Had to be its own crime knowing what kind of man Coleman was.

In June, Dad and Uncle Jack came up with a plan. Said if Uncle Bobby was still alive he'd have already marched up to Coleman and crick'd him in the street. Uncle Bobby was fearless. But this was a delicate matter to cook. That's how Dad says it: cook. Makes them sick to think Coleman's here around all these kids, back and forth from his trailer.

The plan is simple: Uncle Jack, the hunter, crawls into Coleman's trailer when it's dark, when the fireworks have everyone's eyes where they need to be. He's a patient man. He'll wait Coleman out. No different than the pigs on Kerber's farm. Those pigs thought they were clever, too. But Dad and Uncle Jack used to sit up in the barn beams waiting for the fuckers to walk beneath them. When they did, they dropped and wrestled them to the ground. They cut their dicks off later, in the dark, one guy holding the pig's snout shut to keep it from screaming.

I wish Dad never told me anything. No Coleman picking plums. No plan to make him a crick. I wish now that Dynamo was here to talk about swimming in the crick, and Dad and Uncle Jack would laugh about that. I wish I was Blake or Riley sleeping in the grass, exhausted from too much fun, too much playing packed into a single day.

Uncle Jack is smoking cigarettes now, peering from Coleman's trailer window to his feet as if he might cry. I swear he wants it more than Dad. When he found out, he was so pissed, he said, *He's lucky I don't slit his throat.*

By the truck, Libby's pouting and angry and I have an urge to be close to her that moves me in front of her. "Libby," I say so soft it disappears into the oh's and ah's cooing behind us as the fireworks light up the sky, reflecting purple and green off of Libby's tear-wet face.

"What do you want?"

"To talk," I say. "I can get us a beer."

"That's okay," she says, laughing.

"We can take a walk. Stupid fireworks, I swear to—"

"You can leave," Libby says, shutting me up, and I'm so embarrassed and mad I almost say, *I wanted to tell you a secret, about my dad and yours,* but I want to make her feel sorry, too, for brushing me off. I want to run out to the jet field and throw myself to the dogs. And after I've fought them, after I've walked back bloody and brave, she'll see me different.

So I run to the field, where the planes are parked—B52's, Iron Eagles, jets. Even the Hellcat, in the dark, is a sleeping creature, the chrome a mirror gathering firework light. Behind me, Libby's not even looking; she's pouting. I can see Dad loading the cooler up, but he can't see me. Uncle Jack is around back with something in his hands I can't distinguish in the dark. I wonder if I stay out all night, if I hide until the Stealth Bomber fires across the sky, if I can go on pretending they won't do what they plan to do, and Bradley Coleman will go on as some quiet ex-bastard living alone, clean-shaven, with a tomato garden behind his house.

When the finale hits the sky, I bend my neck to watch. I feel, for a moment, like I'm floating, as if watching the colors jump, I can lift into a dream. I nearly fall backwards, but catch myself. I stumble and knock into the dog pen, their constant, though ignored, barking suddenly easing into focus. I can feel something latch onto my ankle.

Takes a minute to realize a pitbull has me. It's a hungry fucker, and at first, I'm tough. I'm shouting, *Goddamn dogs, get off me*, swatting with a fist. But then teeth break my jeans, and I panic. Hurts like Hell. Another one got me above the knee, pulling my legs under the pen. Fireworks are blazing gunshots in the night, aggravating the dogs—the crowd, the park, their cheering. Teeth crawl up my leg, biting into my thighs. I've given up punching. I'm grabbing between my legs to protect myself, and they're biting my hands. The truck is only a hundred feet away. I can see my family, but they're too far to hear me scream. Libby is climbing to the roof, craning her neck to watch the sky explode. Nothing about her says she feels shame, too. Or that she throws up at times, humiliated and scared of my father, like I am of hers. And Dynamo is standing in the bed of the truck, his back to me, firework light turning him into a blinking, iridescent lamp as he raises his arms, and though I can't hear, this is how he'll describe it to me later: that the image of an angel is growing in his memory. She rose from the hills beyond the interstate. Had wings like moonlight and water. And he has to tell someone he's seen God, he knows it. So he stands shouting to Dad and Uncle Jack, to Libby. "I saw an angel," he says. He gives them every detail: her liquid face, the way the sky opened up and accepted her.

Dad and Uncle Jack laugh. "That's no angel, boy. That's a Hellcat," Uncle Jack says. "Got to love the kid, though. Thought the Hellcat was an angel."

And before Dynamo can finish, Uncle Jack pushes his buck knife beside the cooler in the truck and shares a look with Dad, a grave, knowing look like a deep secret Dynamo can never know, and says, "Just like Bobby." His face opening, now, and shedding the hunter, the sniper's eyes, the man that carried, once, his mother bleeding to the couch. "For helicopters and angels; a goddamn sucker." Then he says the girl Uncle Bobby found had bled so much that night he couldn't soak it up. He went for help. He was in the medic's tent when fire lit up the FOB and men poured, it seemed, from the trees, shooting boys dead in their sleep. Bobby crawled to the edge of camp where he'd found the girl in the first place, and hid. Lay listening to the screams, the gunshots, and finally, hours later, the quiet crackle of the tents left burning.

"And don't think that's not brave," Dad says, suddenly, as if that's what he'd wanted Dynamo and the twins and Libby to take away: that Uncle Bobby was no coward, but a good man, and brave. Dynamo doesn't care. He retells his story. He retells with precision. He can feel her still, in his chest. He can see her still, her wings. And it's then, as he spreads his arms like his angel, that Dad spots me behind him, by the pen beneath a pile of pitbulls.

And though I feel only pressure releasing, and arms scooping, I'm told later it took Dad a while to tear me out, that he got his arms all bitten up and bloody, too. But for me, it's only a moment. I can see trailers and trucks bouncing past as Dad says, "You go swimming with dogs, you're bound to get bitten." He's smiling—softer, now, than he had earlier—as if he's thinking I'm no man, but a boy.

CONTRIBUTOR'S NOTES

FELICIA ZAMORA has authored two chapbooks and won the 2015 Tomaž Šalamun Prize (Verse). Her work is found in *Crazyhorse, Meridian, TriQuarterly,* and others. She is an associate poetry editor for the Colorado Review and holds an MFA Colorado State University.

JOSH ENGLISH's work has recently appeared or is forthcoming in journals including *Phantom, Prelude, Sixth Finch, Third Coast* and others. He received his MFA from the University of South Carolina in Columbia where he continues to live and teach.

ELIZABETH SANGER has an MFA in Creative Writing from the University of Montana, and her work has recently appeared or is forthcoming in *Phoebe, Verse Daily, Meridian, TYPO, Conjunctions, Word For/Word, Drunken Boat,* and elsewhere. She currently live in Nashville with her husband and six wildly spoiled cats.

SUZANNE ROSZAK's poetry has appeared or is forthcoming in *Crab Orchard Review, Ecotone, Hayden's Ferry Review, Redivider,* and *ZYZZYVA.* Her first poetry collection, "After the Wake", was a finalist for The University of Wisconsin Press's Brittingham and Pollak Poetry Prizes. Suzanne received her MFA in poetry from The University of California, Irvine.

SIDNEY TAIKO is the Editor-in-Chief of Storm Cellar literary journal. She works for and attends the University of Wisconsin-Milwaukee. She has a crooked spine and a potty mouth, but so far things are working out okay.

DAVID ISHAYA OSU (b. 1991) is a Nigerian poet. He loves to skip and loves to watch water, moon, and rainbow. If he is not writing and sharing poetry, then he is not alive. David has been selected for the 2016 USA Callaloo Creative Writing Workshop.

MORGAN BLALOCK graduates from Hollins University in May 2016. You can find her work in *Prairie Margins, The Adroit Journal, Collision, Mistake House* and more.

ERICA BERNHEIM'S poems, reviews, and interviews have recently appeared or are forthcoming in *DIAGRAM, Forklift, Ohio, Denver Quarterly, The Iowa Review,* and *VOLT,* while her first full-length collection, "The Mimic Sea", was published in 2012 (Indiana University South Bend). She is currently an Associate Professor of English at Florida Southern College, where she also directs the undergraduate creative writing program.

LUKE MUYSKENS was born in Minneapolis, Minnesota, though he now resides in St. Paul, Minnesota. His fiction has appeared in *Superstition Review* and *Digital Americana,* and is forthcoming from *The Hopkins Review.* His poetry has appeared in *New American Writing* and *One Throne Magazine.* He is a second-year MFA candidate in fiction at Queen's University of Charlotte and earned a B.A. from St. John's University. His interests include but are not limited to seltzer water.

VERONICA KUHN is currently an MFA candidate at the University of Virginia. Her poetry has appeared or is forthcoming in *Sonora*

Review, The Adroit Journal, and *DIAGRAM.*

J.R. TORISEVA's work has appeared in, or is forthcoming, from *The North American Review, Salt Hill, The Literary Review, The Saranac Review, The Cincinnati Review, Descant,* and *JACKET,* among others, and included in "Days I Moved Through Ordinary Sound" from *City Lights. Barbed Water,* chosen by Shane McCrae, will be published in 2016 as the winner of Saudade's annual poetry contest. Director of English, Communication and Media Arts, and an Assistant Professor of English at SUNY-GCC, Toriseva has also taught for Mills College, California Poets in the Schools, San Francisco WritersCorps, and Literary Arts of Portland, Oregon.

S.K. STRINGER has short stories published in *Inkwell, Salt Hill,* and *Confrontation,* among others. Currently, she is working on a novel and an essay collection that explores Azerbaijan.

CHRISTOPHER VONDRACEK attended the University of South Dakota for his M.A. in Literature and teaches at Hamline University in Saint Paul. He is writing a memoir on an obsession with Lawrence Welk.

TRACY MAY FUAD is a poet and essayist of Kurdish descent born and raised in Minnesota. Her writing has appeared in *Ninth Letter, BOAAT, Hayden's Ferry Review, DIALOGIST, SOFTBLOW,* and *Nashville Review,* among others. She was in residence at the Vermont Studio Center this spring, and will begin an MFA in Poetry at Rutgers-Newark in the fall.

JENNIFER MURVIN's writing has appeared in *American Short Fiction, The Sun, The Cincinnati Review, Phoebe, Post Road,* and other journals. She was recently the winner of the 2015 American Short(er) Fiction Contest, judged by Stuart Dybek.

MAXIM LOSKUTOFF was raised in western Montana. His stories have appeared in *The Southern Review, The Gettysburg Review, Witness, Narrative,* and *The Chicago Tribune.* A graduate of NYU's MFA program, he was the recipient of a Global Writing Fellowship in Abu Dhabi and the M Literary Fellowship in Bangalore. He has worked as a carpenter, field organizer, bookseller, and writing teacher, among many other things.

LAURA GABEL-HARTMAN is a native Floridian living in the Boston area. Her work has appeared in *Carve Magazine, Feedback,* and *Rio Grande Review.*

DAN PINKERTON lives in Urbandale, Iowa. His stories have appeared in *Green Mountains Review, Washington Square, Quarterly West, Crazyhorse,* and the Best New American Voices anthology.

TERRANCE MANNING, JR. is a graduate from Purdue's MFA in Creative Writing. He's won the Iowa Review Award for Fiction, as well as the Crazyhorse Prize in Nonfiction, and recent work appears in *Witness, Ninth Letter, Boulevard, Southwest Review, Hunger Mountain,* and other magazines. He lives and writes in Pittsburgh, PA.